TIME
TO SAY
GOODBYE

The Case for Getting Quebec out of Canada

REED SCOWEN

M&S

Canadian Cataloguing in Publication Data

Scowen, Reed, 1931–
    Time to say goodbye : the case for getting Quebec out of Canada

Includes bibliographical references.
ISBN 0-7710-7960-5

1. Federal government – Canada.   2. Canada – Politics and government – 1993- .*   3. Quebec (Province) – History – Autonomy and independence movements.   4. Federal-provincial relations – Quebec (Province).   I. Title.

FC98.S365 1999   971.064'8   C99-930992-7
F1034.2.S365 1999

We acknowledge the financial support of the Government of Canada through the Book Publishing Industry Development Program for our publishing activities. We further acknowledge the support of the Canada Council for the Arts and the Ontario Arts Council for our publishing program. Canadä

Set in Minion by M&S, Toronto
Printed and bound in Canada

McClelland & Stewart Inc.
The Canadian Publishers
481 University Avenue
Toronto, Ontario
M5G 2E9

1 2 3 4 5   03 02 01 00 99

CONTENTS

A New Option

On November 15, 1976 – twenty-two years ago as I write these lines – a separatist party was elected to power in the province of Quebec. Since then, Canada's political life has been dominated by the consequences of that vote. The issue has thrown the country into a non-stop debate on constitutional reform. Canada's efforts to satisfy Quebec's aspirations within the framework of our federal system have affected every aspect of government policy. To make matters worse, the debate is rooted in differences between the English and the French, so the conflict has had the effect of heightening tensions between these two language and ethnic groups in Quebec and throughout the country.

Anyone who has been awake for the past twenty years has been obliged to form an opinion on this issue. It may disappear for a few months but we all know it will return. The unity problem has become a chronic affliction, and the purpose of this book is to suggest a way to cure it – to end Quebec's dissatisfaction with the Canadian federation.

Perhaps it's time to ask them to leave.

A lot of people are going to be upset by this proposition. Canadians have poured their energies into the national-unity debate – searching for ways to satisfy Quebec's aspirations, or at least to figure out what they are. And these efforts to reconcile the "Two Founding Peoples" are fuelled by high ideals – fraternity and tolerance. The cause has virtue on its side. And the only alternative is usually referred to as the Break-Up of the country.

Recently the concept of "tough love" has entered our political vocabulary. Some Canadians, frustrated with the lack of progress, are looking at ways to prevent Quebecers from leaving the federation, even if a majority of them were to vote for independence.

There's a lot to be said for keeping Quebec in Canada, either by persuasion or force. Intuitively, it makes sense. But there is another possible way out of the dilemma, a last resort, to be sure, but one that has not had the attention it deserves. We could encourage Quebec to leave, or even insist on it. It's another option – let's call it "Divestiture" – and, under certain circumstances, it might be the best one – for Canada, and for national unity.

In order to get into a frame of mind where this proposition can be looked at calmly, the reader is invited to consider the alternatives. Almost all Canadians have a response, or at least a reaction, to the unity crisis. Perhaps they have never seen the Constitution, but they have read the newspapers and talked to their neighbours. Out of the pain and confusion a number of different viewpoints have evolved, and one way to understand them is in terms of their possible outcomes, of which there are four.

THE OPTIMISTS

Some Canadians believe, or hope, that a new generation in Quebec is turning out to be less interested in the old-fashioned nationalism of its ancestors. They believe that Quebecers are at last ready to take the separatist idea out behind the barn and shoot it. Or if this is not possible then perhaps the issue can be settled in the months ahead, with a constitutional agreement ratified in some way by the people of Quebec and of English Canada. The optimists believe that, one way or another, Quebec will soon be satisfied, and the debate will come to an end.

THE MASOCHISTS

A second view is that the tensions of the national-unity debate are good for us. Supporters of this theory argue that the country was founded on an agreement between two language groups, each based in its own territory. Consequently, Canadians are the administrators of an ethno-linguistic treaty. Perpetual adjustment to the tensions implicit in such an arrangement is the defining feature of our political life. Canada's unique mission among the family of nations is to demonstrate that two great languages and cultures can share the same political space. We should find a way to accept this calling – and enjoy it.

In this group should probably be included a number of people for whom the constitutional debate in Canada has now become a full-time activity – professors, journalists, civil servants, and politicians. They make their living by explaining to us the difference between a "people" and a "society," "sovereignty" and "independence," "federation" and "confederation."

The people who share these beliefs tend to equate the secession of Quebec with the break-up of the country. Their numbers are small but their beliefs are strongly held. Not surprisingly, many of them are to be found in English-speaking Quebec.

THE PRAGMATISTS

A third way of looking at the situation is to see the debate as regrettable, but one that needn't stop us from getting other things done. It's a management problem. From this perspective the unity debate is like the issue of blacks in America, or religion in Ireland – a permanent crevasse in the socio-political landscape of our country. The wisest prime ministers of Canada have always understood that managing this relationship is their most important duty. Pragmatists argue that the best approach is to avoid confrontation by talking about something else whenever possible. They refer to it as a policy of "whistling past the graveyard."

Some of the pragmatists have a more cynical approach. They believe that it's a good idea to keep our politicians occupied with the unity issue, because it leaves them with less time to inflict damage on the economy and meddle in our private lives.

The Fatalists

Finally, there are many English Canadians who see the Quebec problem as a bad thing that is definitely holding us back – a chronic ailment, but one for which there is no cure. It's like arthritis. All that's left is hope, and in the meantime we might try a little magic, a rally, or a student-exchange program. In practical terms, some of these people oppose any more "concessions" to Quebec. Others are willing to let their provincial premiers give it one more try. But they're all prepared to wait and let Quebecers take the initiative – to see if they hold another referendum. If they do, and if this time the vote is "Yes" – then we'll fall off that bridge when we get to it.

These people identify with Joe E. Brown's prayer, "I hope I break even today. I need the money." They are the fatalists, and that attitude seems to represent the way most Canadians feel about the issue today.

Optimist, masochist, pragmatist, fatalist – what's your position on the Quebec question? One way to find out is by establishing an acceptable time frame for its resolution. How much longer are you willing to live with the debate? Forever? For the next twenty years or so? Through one more Quebec referendum? Until we make one last effort at constitutional reform?

Any of these answers would be a good Canadian answer.

But what if you came to the conclusion that the issue could never be resolved – that Quebec could never be satisfied, once and for all, with a transfer of more powers from Ottawa or with a constitutional amendment, no matter how it was worded?

What if you came to the conclusion that Quebec will never vote for complete independence, and yet will never be satisfied with less than independence, because the permanent maintenance of this tension serves its own interests? In other words, what if you believe that there can be no end to the debate, and its economic and social costs, so long as Quebec is part of Canada?

What if you believe that the principle of "Two Founding Nations," "special status," or "distinct society" could never be translated into a meaningful constitutional formula that would be fair and acceptable to all of Canada's provinces and peoples?

What if you were to come to the conclusion that this acrimonious debate is not good for the rest of Canada, but destructive – both practically and psychologically – and seriously diverts us from more vital projects that are essential for the well-being of our people?

Over these past twenty years I've passed through all four stages of understanding – from optimist to masochist to pragmatist to fatalist – and none of them has given satisfaction. So I'd like to take a look at a fifth option. I think it can be argued that the unity debate is a crisis which is so unhealthy, and has such bad effects on the conduct of public policy in Canada, that it should be resolved by Canadians as soon as possible in an active fashion.

And the only solution that will work is Divestiture. It will not mean the break-up of the country. Canada started with four provinces. It got up to ten. We can build a very fine country with nine. This is the alternative we will explore in the pages ahead.

The arguments for Divestiture are based on four premises, which are not generally accepted.

The first premise is that, for reasons of history and demography, Quebecers have fashioned for themselves a political ideology founded on a single, all-encompassing idea. To be credible in Quebec, all political parties, governments, and elected representatives must embrace it. And it's not the idea of independence or separation. It has to do with language, and above all with ethnicity, which some Quebecers prefer to call by the code word "culture." It is the belief that the most important responsibility of the government of Quebec – whether it be a province or an independent state – is to illustrate and strengthen the French language and culture, and to advance the interests of francophones. It resonates throughout Quebec as the "struggle for cultural survival." Quebec is a "nation-state."

It is not only a question of identity. The issue of language and culture has also become for the francophone Quebecer a fabulous political tool for getting and keeping power, both personally and collectively. The unity crisis may have reduced economic opportunity for the average Quebec worker, but it has furnished substantial economic benefits for the province's elite. The tensions created in the rest of Canada by the unity crisis are ideally adapted to the personal objectives of Quebec's leaders and there is no reason for them to change the status quo either by separating or by a final resolution of the issue. In the unity debate, Quebec is playing chess while the rest of Canada is playing checkers.

The second premise is that, in the pursuit of its linguistic goals, Quebec's sense of political identification with Canada, and with

English Canadians, has been undermined to a point where it is irretrievable. For over twenty years every effort at affirmation of the French language and culture in Quebec has been accompanied by a corresponding portrayal of the English – in Quebec, in Ottawa, and in the rest of Canada – as the source of Quebec's problems. As a consequence, Quebec's identification with Canada – an acceptance of its implicit moral code, the desire to participate in its projects and display its symbols – has been terminally eroded. Except in a very limited way, essentially for the economic benefits involved, most Quebecers no longer see themselves as full members of the Canadian community.

This situation has consequences that go far beyond Quebec. Efforts to build a sentiment of fraternity among the diverse peoples and communities of Canada, to achieve a national consensus on issues of public policy, are corroded by this hostility. In this sense, Quebec presents a direct threat to the unity of the entire country, so long as it is a member of the federation.

The third premise is that the rest of Canada is not made up of "nation-states." It is something else, a "civil association," and as such it has no ideology or vocabulary that permits it to engage Quebec in the language debate, or to evolve with Quebec on a collaborative and fruitful basis within a single political unit. The rest of the country has a different vocation. There are no indications that a constitutional solution can be found to reconcile these differences, and there's no point in continuing to debate whether Quebecers are right or wrong. Their cause may be historically understandable, coherent, and convincing – to them. But for the rest of the country it is unacceptable and, ultimately, boring.

The fourth premise, and the most important one, is that Canada's destiny, the Canadian project, should not be limited to an illustration of the concept of "Two Founding Nations" and an unending effort to reconcile their interests within our political structures. It's time to take the pressure off our country. We have been asking it to do the impossible. The frustrations that this issue causes for Canadians outside Quebec are justified. They are unhealthy, and they should be alleviated.

As Canadians we face more important challenges, which are not defined by the languages we speak. Freed from the burden of the Quebec debate, this collective project will become clearer to us all and Canadian unity will be strengthened. And we will not compromise in any way our values of fraternity and tolerance. We can transfer their application to more fruitful ground in a political association that seeks to provide equal opportunity and protection to each person, and is blind to their place of birth and their mother tongue.

These premises are not self-evident. They must be explained. And even if they are accepted, the case for Divestiture must still be made. There are important costs associated with it – economic, social, and psychological. They must be carefully considered – and compared to the corresponding cost of our current policies.

Finally, even if we become convinced of the advantages of Divestiture, a way must be found to do it. How can Quebec be persuaded to leave the federation – and how can Divestiture be accomplished quickly and inexpensively? All of these issues are addressed in the chapters that follow.

It is possible that some readers will remain unconvinced by the arguments for Divestiture. Nonetheless I believe that this option is a serious and realistic one that should become a permanent element of the constitutional debate, and developed further as events unfold in the months ahead. Among its many advantages it provides an opportunity for Canadians to take the initiative with a positive new project of their own, and end the years of simply responding to the latest ultimatum from Quebec City.

2

A Short Note on the Author

Everyone's approach to Canada's national-unity problem is coloured by personal experience. So before we go further I'd like to introduce myself. I'm an English Canadian, born in Quebec, fully bilingual, and I live in Montreal.

Here in Quebec I'm known as an "anglophone." This is a French word, and if you look it up in the *Dictionnaire Larousse* you'll discover that it is just another way of saying "someone who speaks English." But in Quebec it has another meaning. It's a semi-official label, widely used, and applied to people living in Quebec who have English-speaking ancestors. It is a word that reveals your ethnic origin, not the language you speak.

Every Quebecer is either an anglophone, a francophone, or an allophone, which is the name given to people who aren't either French or English. One of the things you have to get used to in Quebec is the daily use of these expressions – by the government, the press, your friends – to explain everything that's going on. Opinion polls on any subject will provide you with the results by ethnic group. Montreal's sports writers keep a close

watch on the playing time allotted to francophone and anglophone players on the local hockey team.

These expressions are applied only to Quebec residents. There
are no "anglophones" outside the borders of this province. The
term is seldom applied to English-speaking people who live in
the other provinces of Canada, and never to the Americans. It's
for internal use only.

It's been said that anglophones and francophones in Quebec
form "Two Solitudes" and that we pass our lives without ever
getting to know each other. I don't think that's true in my case.

I'm not one of the "Westmount Rhodesians" whose carica-
ture energizes the separatist movement. I was born and raised
in a small town, in a part of Quebec that was first settled by the
English. My parents, and four generations of their ancestors,
lived modest lives in small villages of the region. The English
and the French in this part of Quebec, which is known as the
Eastern Townships, have a long tradition of getting along with
each other. Things aren't perfect. As English kids we used to
fight French kids. But there's a lot of mingling and intermar-
riage, and a spirit of tolerance prevails.

When I was growing up, most of the population in the
Townships was English-speaking, so the names of the villages
were English too: East Angus, Bishopton, North Hatley. Since
then the linguistic situation has changed drastically; today 90
percent of the people in this region are French. But a spirit of
collaboration still exists. When a government language police-
man insists that a sign on the "Greg 'n' Roland Restaurant" be
changed to "Restaurant Greg 'n' Roland," questions about his
mental health are raised in both languages.

I didn't speak French fluently as a child, but in my early forties
I decided to get serious about learning the language and immerse
myself fully in the life of the French-speaking community, which,
even then, made up 80 percent of the population of Quebec. No

one could say that my efforts were half-hearted. In fact I became one of a very small number of English-speaking Quebecers – a couple of dozen over the past twenty years – who decided to make a full-time career in Quebec politics and public life.

A few months after René Lévesque and the Parti Québécois came to power in 1976, I was elected to the Quebec National Assembly, as a Liberal, in the Montreal constituency of Notre-Dame-de-Grâce (N.D.G.). The riding is about equally divided between French and English residents. I was their member of the National Assembly for ten years, through three elections. During those years I worked almost exclusively in French. Members of the Quebec Legislature have the right to speak in English, thanks to the Canadian Constitution. They can, but they don't, for the simple reason that almost no one listening or watching on television would understand what was being said. So, for the most part, we speak French.

My ten years in politics were exciting. We did all the things they do in the other provincial legislatures of Canada, but we also had a referendum on independence in 1980. And some very controversial language legislation (known locally as Bill 101) was adopted and amended several times. It was a turbulent period in Quebec – and for Canada as well. There were many long days and nights spent in Quebec City. I got to know all my fellow actors in the drama. René Lévesque and I tended to get on each other's nerves. But I got along very well with some other members of the PQ government: Jacques Parizeau, Gérald Godin, Pierre-Marc Johnson, Rodrigue Biron, Bernard Landry, Yves Duhaime, to name only a few. It also goes without saying that, in the Liberal Party, most of my colleagues were French-speaking. Some of them have remained friends to this day. And I visited every corner of Quebec province in those ten years, during election and referendum campaigns, and for party conferences.

When the Liberals won the 1985 election I became senior economic advisor and parliamentary assistant to the premier,
Robert Bourassa, and worked in his office for the following two
years. After leaving politics I continued to work from 1987 to
1995 within the Quebec bureaucracy, mainly in French, as the
province's *délégué generale* in London and New York City.

So that makes about twenty years of full-time involvement in
the public life of Quebec, not just as an interested observer, but
as a French-speaking participant. I still don't qualify as a francophone, and never will, but I think I know quite a bit about
what's going on in francophone Quebec.

I've been outspoken and visible in the positions I've defended
in my public life. One of the first things I did after getting
elected was to prepare a manifesto on the role of the English in
Quebec,[1] and since then I've been speaking and writing, more or
less non-stop, on the economic, linguistic and constitutional
policies of Quebec and Canada. Most of what I have had to say
has been generously received – and frequently accepted – by
both French and English Quebecers.

I want to make it clear that even if I'm taking a look at ways
to get Quebec out of the Canadian federation it's not because I
don't like it here, or because I harbour any regrets about my
experience in the public life of this province. I've had a good
time doing some useful things.

It's also important to understand that the only thing I am
talking about in this book is politics. For most of us this is a
subject that occupies only a small corner of our lives. The really
important preoccupations, joys, and disappointments of life are
to be found in other places. Family, friends, work, religion,
recreation, the arts, the media – these are the things that really
define who we are. Even in Quebec, where the state takes an
unusually active interest in our "collective identity," there is a
host of private pleasures and opportunities to be enjoyed. If

Quebec were no longer a province of Canada it could still be a very acceptable place to live, and Montreal and the Laurentian Mountains would be as easy to visit and enjoy as they are today.

So I'm not fed up with Quebec, or Quebecers – far from it. It's where I live and I've already made a reservation in the North Hatley cemetery. This book is just about politics, in a federal system.

During my years in public life I was too often obliged to choose between Quebec and Canada. Having chosen to work for the Quebec government I usually gave priority to Quebec's interests. But to see an aquarium, it's better not to be a fish. Since leaving politics I've been living in London and New York. More recently my work has taken me to every part of Canada. This change in my environment, and the passage of time, have led me to reconsider some of the things I did during those years in Quebec politics. For instance, I voted against Pierre Trudeau's repatriation of the Constitution in 1982, and for the Meech Lake Accord, with its "distinct society" clause, in 1987. I was convinced I was acting in the best interests of Quebec, although most of the people in my constituency didn't agree. Now I'm not so sure I was right.

I've also begun to reflect in a different way on what I learned during these past twenty years. While doing that, I seem to have rediscovered Canada. But the path to this new understanding surely began in Quebec.

3

A Shocking Revelation

Quebec is a nation-state. This was not always clear to me. In the '60s, living in Montreal, I watched the growth of Quebec nationalism – the FLQ, the language debates. But it was not until early in 1977 that my own life was touched by it.

At the time I was a member of the Quebec civil service, but working in Ottawa, on loan to the federal government's Anti-Inflation Board. A few weeks earlier, a separatist party, the Parti Québécois, had been elected to form the government of Quebec. It seemed obvious that interesting and important things were about to happen in my province and I wanted to be involved. So I flew back to Quebec City and called on Louis Bernard, the *chef du cabinet* of the new premier of Quebec, René Lévesque. Bernard was about to become secretary of the Executive Council, the most important civil servant of the Quebec government, and I asked him to reintegrate me into the public service.

His answer was surprisingly clear. He told me he thought I should resign, because there was no more place for anglophones in the Quebec civil service.

Please keep in mind that my conversation with Louis Bernard was in French. I spoke French, but to the new government he represented, I was an "anglophone." And consequently, a career in the public service of my own province was no longer possible. With several generations of family history in Quebec behind me, this came as a big surprise.

I've never forgotten that meeting. It was on Friday, January 14, 1977, and it was my first intimation that Quebec nationalism might have personal consequences. This didn't discourage me. I remember thinking that Bernard could be speaking only for his government. Surely this simplistic effort at ethnic discrimination could not possibly reflect the views of the Quebec people.

So I set out to prove him wrong. When I walked out of his office I didn't leave the province or decide to grumble from the sidelines. I got involved, full time, for the next eighteen years, as an anglophone in the public life of Quebec. However, what I discovered is that Mr. Bernard was right. And it's not just his political party that feels this way. French-speaking Quebecers see no reason to have anglophones in the civil service. And so, today, there aren't any. I also discovered that this impulse to limit and reduce the dimensions of the anglophone community goes far beyond the question of representation in the bureaucracy. Despite an unending litany of ritual declarations of respect for its "historic rights," the anglophone community of the province has been so narrowly defined and so tightly regulated in the laws which restrict its activities that it is declining and can only continue to decline. These restrictions are supported by the only two political parties that matter in Quebec, for the simple reason that practically all French Quebecers, certainly all those with influence in these matters, want it to be that way.

My own interest in advancing the cause of an autonomous English-speaking community within Quebec, and of Quebec's continuing presence within Canada, came to an end on the evening of October 30, 1995, when the premier of the province singled out the "ethnic" citizens of his province and blamed them for the defeat of his independence project. He later justified these remarks as a piece of socio-political analysis. But on that referendum night Mr. Parizeau was not appearing as a professor. He was speaking as premier of all the people of Quebec. And his statement was a touching reminder that nothing had changed in the previous twenty years. It's important not to make too much of this incident or of my visit to Louis Bernard in 1977. They are illustrations only. But they serve as neat bookends for the story I'm about to tell.

My goal when I began this adventure twenty years ago was to ensure that the members of the English community would continue to have a place in the province they had called home for many generations – as Canadians. In the face of a tidal wave of French nationalism I was still dreaming of a bilingual Quebec.

A bilingual Quebec is a place where the two languages – one essential internally, the other just as necessary on this continent – are treated with equal respect by the state and the public sector. It's not a linguistic homeland. In a bilingual Quebec the government accepts responsibility for maintaining an equilibrium between the two languages. There could be some efforts to encourage the French language, to offset the very powerful attraction of English. But this would be done on a collaborative basis, in consultation with the English community. Such an equilibrium is difficult to achieve. It requires constant adjustment. It has to be sanctioned by the state and valued by all citizens as an important moral bond between them. And its benefit, apart from the pleasures of English pubs and French cafés, could be a more tolerant, sophisticated, and open society – a better place to live.

The foundation was in place. The English in Quebec had created, over many years, a distinct community, supported by a full range of educational, cultural, and health institutions, and businesses that functioned in the English language. There was nothing immoral in this. Surely it was not necessary to dismantle this community to provide more space for French. Could not one group expand without forcing the other to contract?

The French argued that their minorities in the rest of Canada had even fewer "privileges" than the English enjoyed in Quebec. But for English Quebecers this comparison was irrelevant. Their alternative to living in this province was not to live in French in Manitoba. If the English were to remain in Quebec we would have to keep conditions reasonably competitive with the kind of life they could live, in English, elsewhere in Canada or in the U.S.A.

I don't think that I had it all worked out so clearly in 1977. It was more a feeling then, a feeling that we could have, in Montreal, what we had in the Eastern Townships when I was a child: an understanding that there were both French and English people in our community, that we were different, but that we both belonged there. I believed that we could retain this understanding, and make it work in Montreal as well.

If I was going to work for a competitive climate for English Quebecers, it seemed clear that there were two connected problems to be addressed: the future of the English in Quebec, and the future of Quebec in Canada. On both issues it was French Quebec that had seized the initiative. The rest of us were supposed to respond. I decided to be part of that response.

The conclusion I have come to, after two decades of full-time engagement, is that Quebec is not a community that a significant number of English-speaking people would choose as a place to live, work, and raise a family. This will not change because it's the way the French-speaking majority wants things to be.

There are quite a few people in Quebec's English-speaking community who think I was a very slow learner, that it should not have taken me eighteen years to make these discoveries. In fact, from my very first hours in politics I was besieged by adversaries in the anglophone community who insisted that I was wasting my time. Many more didn't bother to argue with me; they simply cleared out. However, even today, there are some English-speaking Quebecers who say that two decades is not enough, and that we should keep trying.

I'll tell you my story. You decide for yourself.

4

Bill 101: Claude Ryan to the Rescue!

For the two years after leaving Mr. Bernard's office, a number of commitments kept me in Ottawa, but in the autumn of 1978 I found myself in Quebec, in politics, and in the middle of a superheated debate between the French and the English over political and economic power, thinly veiled behind the romantic vocabulary of cultural *épanouissement*. I was face to face with Bill 101.[1]

THE BACKGROUND TO BILL 101

Since at least 1976 nearly all French-speaking Quebecers, separatists and federalists alike, have agreed on two things. They want more constitutional and political power for Quebec, and less for Ottawa. They want more power than is available to Canada's other provinces – a "special status" or "sovereignty-association." They justify this demand with one argument only: the need to protect and strengthen the French language and culture. Separatists insist on total control while federalists seek recognition as a "distinct society." But the basic impulse is the same: you are English, we are French; we want to govern ourselves.

What would be the effect of a further transfer of constitutional powers to Quebec? No one knows for sure. However, we can imagine it by taking a look at what successive Quebec governments have done to expand the French language and culture over the past two decades with the powers they already have. The present situation would, logically, be the starting point for further gestures of self-affirmation.

From the beginning of Quebec's Quiet Revolution,[2] one possibility for strengthening the French language, certainly the most civilized one, was to encourage its use through positive action. In theory, at least, more French does not require less English. However, during the '60s a consensus developed in Quebec around the belief that positive action alone would not work, that the attractions of English were too strong. Practical considerations, fuelled by a deep-seated urge to avenge past injustices, led to a decision that the space occupied by the English language in Quebec must be reduced, by law, to provide more space for French.

The entire French-speaking population of Quebec, urban and rural, young and old, rich and poor, agrees with this line of reasoning. For twenty years the language debate in Quebec has not been about whether there should be legislation to limit the use of English, only about how far it should be taken.

Turkeys don't vote for Thanksgiving. The English in Quebec were instinctively opposed to language legislation. And when Bill 101 was adopted in 1977, many of them simply moved out of the province. However, a surprisingly large number of the more influential members in the community were sympathetic to the fears of their French-speaking neighbours, and were ready to give language legislation a chance, provided it was implemented in a spirit of compromise.

In an earlier book I have told the story of how this compromise was worked out.[3] The "anglophones" were taken by surprise. They had always thought of themselves simply as English Canadians living in Quebec, and it had never occurred to them that they might have to get organized as a locally based minority linguistic group. They had never even thought of themselves linguistically. But in order for Quebec's majority to become "francophones," the English-speaking people of the province were requested to become "anglophones."

Some prominent members of the English community accepted this invitation and, over a few years, developed a definition of both the space and the institutions that would be essential to the community's continued existence and growth. The anglophones involved in this exercise were not attempting to invent Paradise, just an environment that would be reasonably competitive with Toronto and the rest of North America as a place for English-speaking people to live. The details of this compromise proposal – these limits to the restrictions on the use of English that would provide the anglophone community with the space necessary to maintain itself in Quebec – have been known and understood for at least fifteen years.

It was clear from the beginning that the separatist party, which had conceived Bill 101, would have no interest in amending it. So, in response to an unequivocal promise of support from the English-speaking community, the Liberal Party of Quebec promised that, when elected, they would change Quebec's language laws to ensure this new equilibrium between the French and English communities. But the promise was never kept, even during the nine years from 1985 to 1994 when the Liberal Party was in power, for the simple reason that the required measures are not supported by the French-speaking community.

I was directly involved in this language debate for eighteen years, as a member of the National Assembly, and later as chairman of Alliance Quebec, an interest group representing the English community.

THE MAN OF PRINCIPLE

When I was first elected to the National Assembly in 1978, the Liberals were in opposition to the Parti Québécois government. And they had a new leader, Claude Ryan. Quebec federalists were rallying around him as the man who could challenge the separatist government, defeat its proposed referendum on independence, and win the next provincial election.

The federalist forces had been dazed by the election of René Lévesque in 1976 and it was in this loopy condition that they chose Ryan as their leader. No one was ever less suited to political life and he turned out to be one of the great tragicomic figures of modern Quebec politics. A professional journalist with a quick mind and a wicked sense of humour, he could be every bit as emotional as his great adversary René Lévesque. But, unlike Lévesque, he insisted that there was an intellectual and moral justification for all of his declarations, no matter how contradictory they seemed. And, unlike most politicians, he liked to put it all in writing. Ryan also believed that he occupied a moral high ground that lesser mortals could only dream of. Long before professional boxers and football players began to credit divine intervention for their success, Ryan was telling his followers that he was guided by the "Hand of God" in the development of his policies. The existence of this link, and speculation on the nature of the relationship, inspired much merriment among Quebec journalists.

Liberals first began to have second thoughts about their new leader after a famous speech in Lennoxville in which he announced the twelve conditions that would apply to anyone seeking nomination as an official Liberal candidate. Ryan declared that he would associate himself only with those whose finances, and physical and mental health, were in good shape, and whose private lives were "honourable and irreproachable." Aspirants were also to possess "irreproachable professional and civic integrity," a "trained intellect," and be "capable of independent intellectual activity." Anyone seeking "personal advancement" would not be welcome.

I remember feeling distinctly relieved that I had been elected before these new rules came into effect. The press had a field day assessing me and my colleagues in the light of the new criteria. But, in any event, reality intervened and as a happy member of the group of reprobates, sinners, and self-seekers who finally got nominated as Liberals to run in the 1981 elections, I was delighted to learn that Ryan was proud of us after all. He still had his principles, but they were new principles. He declared that we had been democratically chosen in each constituency and were true representatives of the people.

This experience should have prepared me for the dizzying array of positions on the language issue that Ryan was to come up with in the years ahead. The same person who argued in 1978 that Bill 101 "abusively forbade" the use of English on signs was able to vote for the continuation of this ban in 1988 because he had just discovered the "profound attachment of Quebec's francophones for Bill 101."[4] And when Ryan became Minister of Education he flatly repudiated the promises he had made in 1979 on access to English schools.

It's perhaps unfair to single out Claude Ryan for his inconsistencies on the language question. In fact, most of the federalist elite in Quebec display a similar ambivalence. In their heads they understand that the English have a right to be treated as full members of Quebec society. In their hearts they think it might be easier for everyone if these same English stopped whining and accepted the status quo, or got out of town.

But from the beginning of the debate, Ryan was the one person who made the principles involved very clear. He defined, in writing, an acceptable compromise between the French and the English in Quebec. He was unable to get himself elected as premier. But, for a time at least, as a very influential minister in the Bourassa government of 1985, he was in a position to put many of his promises and principles into practice. Unfortunately, he had second thoughts. The English put their trust in a messiah who was out of town on Judgement Day.

The Liberal Promise

But I digress. The starting point in the search for a political solution to the dilemma of the English community in Quebec was the summer of 1978. The event was the first by-election to take place after René Lévesque and the Parti Québécois came to power, in the Montreal riding of Notre-Dame-de-Grâce (N.D.G.). It was Ryan's first political test, and it was mine as well, for I had been chosen as the official candidate of the Liberal Party.

In that by-election there was only one issue on the agenda. A few months earlier, the government had adopted the Charter of the French Language (popularly known as Bill 101), the most comprehensive piece of legislation ever sanctioned, in a democracy, to promote the use of one language by limiting the use of another. The stated intention of Bill 101 was to make French "the language of government and the law as well as the normal and everyday language of work, instruction, communication, commerce and business."[5] To accomplish this, it severely restricted access to English schools, forbade the use of English on public signs, and limited its use in the workplace.

At the time, the voters of N.D.G. were mainly English and they saw Bill 101 as a declaration of war on their community.

The legislation acknowledged that there were English in Quebec. But should their community continue to be allowed to remain, live, work, and grow, in English? The answer, made explicit in both the tone and substance of Bill 101, was *No way!* This law was the cornerstone – in fact, the entire foundation – on which the Quebec nation-state was to be constructed.

The issue posed a very practical problem for the Liberal candidate in N.D.G. In reaction to Bill 101, a new party, Freedom of Choice, had been formed. Its policy was that there should be no language legislation at all. At the time the population of the riding was mainly anglophone, and so the notion had a certain appeal. The Liberal Party needed its own policy on language, and fast, if we were going to win the by-election.

The voters in N.D.G. were not the only ones interested in hearing what the new Liberal leader would say on the language issue. For nearly a decade everyone in the province had been following the Liberal Party's tortured efforts to reconcile Quebec's nationalist passions with the principles of liberal democracy. The inherent contradictions had cost the previous leader, Robert Bourassa, his job as premier, and the party membership continued to be bitterly divided on the issue. Bourassa had been accused of having no principles. Ryan had many, and he promised to sort the problem out for us, once and for all.

Ryan asked me to draft a new policy on the place of English in Quebec, basing it on a document on the subject which he had prepared for his own leadership campaign a few months earlier,[6] and on the ideas that the leaders of the English community had been developing. This would give us a program we could use in the by-election campaign.

Reading Ryan's document, I was encouraged to believe that Louis Bernard was wrong, that there could be a place for anglophones in Quebec after all. Ryan's manifesto did not actually talk of a bilingual community, but in the context of the times it went a long way in that direction. He said the English community had "the right to an open and explicit legal recognition." He defined the English community broadly, including anyone who was educated in that language "regardless of their place of birth." And he promised to allow English on signs, widen access to English schools, and provide provincial and municipal services, including health care and social services, in English on request. So it took only a few telephone conversations between us before the new, and official, Liberal policy on language was sent to the printer.[7] It was prominently displayed during the N.D.G. by-election and again a few months later in a second by-election, when Ryan himself was the Liberal candidate.

In this way Quebec's anglophone community defined the conditions necessary to keep its province competitive with Ontario, Alberta, and the U.S.A. as a place for English-speaking people to live. The Liberal Party promised to create these conditions if elected to power. The same commitments (with very minor modifications) were still in the party program seven years later when the Liberals finally won a general election and could, at last, put them into effect.[8]

5

A Competitive English Community

The new policies that were promised represented a compromise, inspired by some big changes in the mindset of Quebec's anglophones. In 1975 we had been the oppressors. Two years later we had become the oppressed. Nowhere else in the world has an English-speaking community been obliged to establish the conditions for its survival as an indigenous minority group. Our problem was complicated by the existence of adjacent regions where English-speaking people could live without having to think about their language. And Bill 101 had been designed by an adversary armed with bound volumes of the absolute truth.

We needed space for an English community to be English in a way that its members would determine. Some limitations could be accepted because of the other attractions of Quebec. One of these, if we got it right, might even include participation in a unique and harmonious community of two languages and cultures. But people would have to be allowed to live here, in English, to the extent that they wanted, or many of them would leave. What emerged after much consultation was a short list of essential conditions.

Let's take a look at these promised conditions – and at what happened to them.

THE DEFINITION OF THE COMMUNITY

Believe it or not, the first issue that arises is one of definition. Who is an English Quebecer? For most observers outside the province the answer would be simple: anyone who is speaking English in Quebec. And one might reasonably expect that people would be left free to make that decision for themselves.

Unfortunately it's not that easy. If you are going to have laws that permit but limit the use of English, it's necessary to decide who is eligible. So a number of definitions of the English have come into existence and they all define the community in a narrow way.

The Canadian census, ideology free, uses four definitions to calculate the size of the English language group in Quebec. They produce quite different answers to the question, "How many anglophones live in Quebec?" (Figures based on 1996 census.)[1]

Quebecers who say they speak only English	358,505
Quebecers whose mother tongue is English (the language first learned and still understood)	586,435
Quebecers whose "home language" is English (the language most frequently used in the home)	710,970
Quebecers who say they have a knowledge of English	3,195,725
Total Quebec population	7,045,085

In its efforts to restrict the use of English, the Quebec government began with the premise that membership in the anglophone community should be limited to those whose mother tongue is English. Today they number 586,000, a decrease of about 215,000, or 27 percent, since the Parti Québécois was elected for the first time in 1976.[2] In that year, the English made up 13 percent of Quebec's population; the figure is now down to about 8 percent. This is the measure of the anglophone exodus which has cost the community some of its most mobile and productive members.

The engineering of Quebec's project to reduce the importance of its English community began with the identification of the anglophone as someone who was born in that language, rather than as someone who can speak it. This step eliminated roughly 1.6 million people who say they have a knowledge of English, including 125,000 who use it as their normal language. The process was further refined with a second, brilliantly conceived, definition: "*les anglophones de souche*." This expression translates roughly as "English who have been here a long time," or who are "of old stock." People meeting this test are now the only members of the English community for whom both Quebec's political parties are willing to accept some responsibility.

The number of generations of Quebec ancestry required for membership in this group has never been specified. But one thing is clear: if you speak English but you weren't born in Quebec, you are not an *anglophone de souche*, regardless of your mother tongue, and the government would prefer that you live in French. The same attitude applies to the children of *anglophones de souche*, born in the '80s and '90s. The expression also excludes anyone speaking English who has arrived recently, and all those who may come in the future. Considering the mobility of English-speaking people in Canada, it excludes perhaps one-third of the anglophones who are living in Quebec at the present time. Both political parties constantly refer to *anglophones de souche* when defining those who should have the right to be English in Quebec. "If you don't have roots you don't have rights" is the prevailing sentiment towards those who want to live in English in Quebec.

Defining the community in these terms is a polite way of putting an end to it over time. It's a group one can resign from, but no new members will be accepted. There are perhaps 400,000 people in Quebec today who would qualify as *anglophones de souche*.[3] They were born there in English and it is proposed to allow them to die in the same language. But both political parties argue that all newcomers, and young English Quebecers, have a civic duty to integrate into the French community. It's clear that acceptance of this definition puts a kind of pressure on the critical mass of the community which will lead to the gradual disappearance of English-language institutions.

Two specific applications of this narrow definition can be found in the legislation on education and immigration.

Education. In Quebec, access to English-language schools is tightly controlled. It is taken for granted that no francophone can make use of them. Only if you are a Canadian citizen educated in Canada and in English do your children have the right to attend an English school.

The Liberals promised to relax this restriction and open English schools to all English-speaking children, "regardless of their place of birth,"[4] and, presumably, regardless of their parents' citizenship. When in power they refused to implement this promise. It was decided that all parents educated in English outside Canada – in the United States or the U.K. for instance – must send their children to French schools. The policy of the Parti Québécois is even more restrictive. It states that you can't go to an English school unless your parents were educated in English – in Quebec. Their policy has not been implemented only because the Canadian Constitution will not allow it.

The result of these limitations on access to schools can be

imagined. Since 1978, the English-school population has declined by 60 percent, from 250,000 to 100,000.[5] There are now more French-language schools in Ontario than English schools in Quebec.[6]

Immigration. The policy of both the Liberal Party and the Parti Québécois is that all immigrants arriving in the province have come not to Canada but to Quebec. Even those whose first language is English are expected to integrate into the franco-phone community. In the selection process, fifteen points are accorded to the candidate for a knowledge of French, two for a knowledge of English.[7] On arrival, all successful candidates are encouraged to participate in a very effective program designed to ensure their agreement to a "moral contract with the host society." The society described to them is not Canada, it's Quebec. Furthermore, no provision is made for an allocation in the immigration quotas to enrich the English community and encourage its growth. Everyone in Quebec whose first language is neither English nor French – Chinese and Italian alike – has a duty to assimilate into the French community.

As one might imagine, this policy has not made Quebec a popular point of entry for immigrants. Only about 12 percent of the Canadian total comes to this province.[8] But it has ensured that those who do come will integrate into the French community.

ENGLISH IN THE PUBLIC ADMINISTRATION

The most critical single factor in keeping a healthy English-speaking community in Quebec is its representation in the public service. If English-speaking Quebecers are to feel they are a part of Quebec society, it's axiomatic that they must see themselves reflected in their own public administration. More important, and at a very practical level, the financing and administration of the province's schools and hospitals is now almost completely controlled by the provincial government. If English Quebecers are to retain the right to manage their own institutions, much of this management will have to be done from within the public service.

So Robert Bourassa and the Liberal Party were elected in 1985 after having made a very specific promise to "increase the representation of anglophones in the public and para-public service to a level which reflects the numerical importance of this group."[9] At the time, this would have required that the presence of English Quebecers be established at about 10 percent. There was no doubt that this could be done if the political will existed. We had an excellent model to follow in Ottawa.

It was in response to a similar imbalance that Pierre Trudeau, in 1968, undertook to increase the representation of French-speaking Canadians in the federal public service. A permanent commission was created to address the problem. Specific goals with target dates were established. Free courses in French were offered. Bilingual civil servants were rewarded with bonuses and preference for promotions. Many senior posts were limited to those who were bilingual. As a result of these measures, well over half of all public servants in Ottawa, including those at the highest levels, can now work in French.

During the nine years that the Quebec Liberal Party was in power from 1985 to 1994, nothing was done to respect the promise to increase the levels of English in the civil service. As a result there are now virtually no anglophones employed in the public service of Quebec. The official figure in 1997 was 411 out of 51,000, or 0.8 percent of the total.[10] Of the thousand or so Order-in-Council appointments to the government's numerous Crown corporations, boards, and commissions, virtually none go to anglophones. There are 150 deputy and associate deputy ministers in the Quebec government. Two of them are anglophones.[11]

For the English-speaking community, the Quebec government is "their" government, not "ours." This situation is a direct consequence of the policies of both the Liberals and the Parti Québécois. There is no support among French-speaking Quebecers for any change in this policy.

ENGLISH IN THE HEALTH AND SOCIAL-SERVICE NETWORKS

In attempting to establish the minimum conditions for a competitive English community, it was quickly agreed that the existence of English institutions for the sick, the elderly, and the poor is essential. Twenty-five years ago, an impressive network of these was in place, created over many decades by English-speaking Quebecers, who staffed them and controlled their destinies. They included large city hospitals, such as the Royal Victoria and the Jewish General, regional medical centres in such cities as Quebec City and Sherbrooke, child-support services, residences for the elderly and handicapped, and home-care services.

The language laws adopted in 1977 swept all these institutions up into one French-language regime. They were told to give themselves French names, communicate with the government – and anyone else who made the request – in French, keep their records in French, allow all employees to work in French and, except in municipalities where the English made up over 50 percent of the population, to post all signs in French only. In other words, there were to be no more English institutions in the publicly funded health and social-services systems, only a limited number of institutions that could offer their services in English if requested.

The Liberal Party promised to change all this. They not only agreed that the English community should regain control of its hospitals and social-service centres, they made the commitment that "a Liberal government will guarantee to the English-language community the right to the orientation and the administration of its educational, cultural, health and social service institutions."[12]

The commitment was forgotten the day after the Liberals were elected. The English institutions were not returned to the English community. The only gesture in this direction during the nine years of Liberal administration was the adoption of a law to oblige a limited number of institutions to provide some specific services in English. The policy has still not been implemented because employees of the centres affected insist that they cannot be obliged to speak English at work.

At the present time, 70 of the 553 health and social-service institutions in Quebec are designated as "bilingual."[13] There is not a single health or social-service centre in the province that is designated as English, and that the English community has the right to "orient and administrate" in its own language.

The Visible Face of Quebec

The feature of Quebec's language laws that is most notorious outside the province, and around the world, is the requirement that all public signs, indoors and outdoors, large and small, lit and unlit, be in French, and, with very few exceptions, in French only. Even traffic signs come under its jurisdiction – to the dismay of visitors who find themselves heading down the wrong side of an autoroute.

This aspect of the language law, and its bizarre application in specific cases, has been a bonanza for stand-up comics all over North America. Inside Quebec it's the one that the English community has objected to most strenuously, as being insulting, and an infringement of individual rights.

I have described the debates over this issue in an earlier

book.[14] For our purposes it is important simply to note that both political parties, and virtually all members of the French-speaking community, think these regulations are a good thing. It was this pressure of popular opinion that persuaded the Liberal Party not to respect its promise to allow bilingual signs when elected to power. Even when obliged to do so by a Supreme Court decision in 1988, it refused, in the interests of "social peace."

Two years later the Liberal government adopted a minor modification to the law, which permitted a limited amount of English wording on signs under tight restrictions. However, each time members of the English community ask retailers to implement these legal changes, they are branded as radicals and accused of threatening the same "social peace." The Liberal Party says that the English are being "irresponsible." The Parti Québécois spokesperson says that if the English insist that this law be respected, the government should change it.

So signs in Quebec remain, to all intents and purposes, in French only (84 percent in Montreal in 1997),[15] and that's the way the French-speaking population wants it to be. In 1996, the language police responded to an average of fifteen complaints per day about English wording in stores. The current Liberal Party policy is that the sign laws have "established a balance of linguistic peace which should not be disturbed."[16] The Parti Québécois would disturb it only to further restrict the use of English.[17]

ENGLISH AT WORK

It's when you try to get a job in Quebec that you begin to understand that a francophone is not just someone who can speak French.

The official purpose of Quebec's language law is to make French the "normal and everyday language of work."[18] It states that "workers have a right to carry on their activities in French"[19] and prohibits an employer from making knowledge of English a condition in hiring unless it can be proven that English is essential for the job. The law requires that all professional corporations operate in French only and that all members of a professional group have a working knowledge of French. A doctor or nurse who speaks only English may not operate a practice or be employed in this province, even if their intention is to serve only an English clientele. Any company with more than fifty employees must first install French-language programs in its computers, then seek special permission from the Office of the French Language if workers request software in another language.[20]

These laws speak of a language of work, but from the beginning everyone understood that they were talking about a "people." The province's most important employer group, the Conseil du Patronat, made this crystal clear. In its brief on Bill 101 it stated: "The Conseil is in agreement with the basic idea of a concerted effort by the state, businesses and citizens to *promote the use of French* in Quebec and to make it the main language in economic and cultural activities. But the concrete goal of the Conseil, through the promotion of French, is, first and foremost, *the promotion of francophones*. The majority of Quebecers are francophones and it's their welfare and their progress which the Conseil intends to advance."[21] (My emphasis.)

The Conseil du Patronat, it should be noted, is a federalist group and most of its members support the Liberal Party.

The policy has been carried out across the board. Professional service firms – legal and accounting – have come to understand that the ability to communicate in French is not enough; there must be francophone names on the letterhead. Every important company in the province continues to make a distinction between the ability to speak French and "being French" when making important appointments. It's often pointed out that political uncertainty has a negative effect on the Quebec economy. But it has had a very positive effect on the francophone share of that economy. It is a form of economic protection more powerful than anything dreamed up in Ottawa for our farmers and magazine publishers.

Quebec is not the first or the only place in the world where race, colour, and the name of your school can affect your prospect of getting a job. Its distinct contribution to this kind of discrimination is a tacit encouragement of the practice by the government, made manifest in the objectives and the rhetoric of its language legislation.

If Quebec were a closed economy, the past twenty years of state intervention, reinforced by an unspoken pressure on firms to employ francophones, would have been sufficient to eliminate anglophones from the workplace of the province. However, the English in the rest of Canada and the United States have, unwittingly, come to the rescue by refusing to do business with Quebec companies in French. The department-store buyer in Toronto who orders Quebec-made furniture, like the Hollywood movie producers who use Quebec-designed software, is unconcerned with the province's delicate sensibilities in language matters, and wants to talk to somebody who speaks English. And so do the tourists.

Consequently, there is still a lot of English being spoken, in Montreal at least. But it's not because of any agreement between the English and the French. The officially encouraged mindset of the French-speaking population is that everyone who lives in Quebec should work in French, switching to English only when an outsider requires it, and that preference in hiring should be given to francophones.

A *FAIT ACCOMPLI*

What I have described here is the systematic weakening of a minority-language community through the use of a legislation that is supported by all elements of the majority community for its own benefit. An effort was made by the leaders of the English community to find a compromise and an agreement was reached. But it was not respected. The right to membership in the English community has been defined ever more narrowly, in the law and on the street. The English are totally without representation in the public service of Quebec. Commitments were made to widen access to their schools, to leave them to run their own health institutions, to leave them free to use their own language on public signs. None of these promises has been kept.

The leaders of the English community who dreamed up this compromise in the late '70s have nearly all retired from the nerve-wracking fray, exhausted or fed up, many of them discredited by their own community for their naïveté. Three of the best – Rick French, Clifford Lincoln, and Herb Marx – were lost in a single day in 1988, when they resigned as cabinet ministers on a matter of principle over the signs issue.

The entire French-speaking population of Quebec has observed this process for twenty years and has approved, or remained silent. By way of comparison, Pierre Trudeau's effort to increase the use of French in Ottawa and across the country was made possible by significant support from Canada's English-speaking community. In Quebec, no member of the francophone leadership in the business, academic, cultural, or social communities has ever chosen to criticize the language legislation or to be identified with the anglophone project. The bridge was built but there was no one on the other side.

Quebec francophones who identify themselves as federalists

have repeatedly asked the English community not to insist that the promises be kept, because it helps the separatist cause or "threatens the social peace." It's important to understand the meaning of this expression, which has nothing to do with "peace" and everything to do with politics. The argument goes as follows: "We did make that promise. But we Liberals are already seen as the party of the English establishment. If we make these changes now there will be social unrest, which will encourage more undecided Quebecers to vote for the Parti Québécois. Do you want another referendum?" This mantra has been repeated within the Liberal caucus, at party conventions and in the press, since that party took power in 1985. And it's probably true. If the language laws were modified to provide space for a healthy English community in Quebec, a majority of the population would vote for independence. They would certainly not vote for the Liberal Party.

The Liberal Party declares that the current language policies have established "social peace." But peace comes in different forms. One kind is the fruit of an agreement freely arrived at. Another is silence, imposed when one side is too strong to be resisted. Currently we have the second kind. The Liberal promises have not been kept, and there is no coherent or credible leadership in the English community today to mount a resistance. As a consequence, even before Quebec has obtained new constitutional powers to reinforce its French identity, the province's English-speaking community lives within a structure of restrictions that guarantees its continuing decline.

But the English, unlike many minority groups around the world, have options. They can move a few miles east or west or south and put all this behind them. So Quebec's English community is slowly declining in numbers and in strength. Its essential institutions are being eroded. The result is a political climate that is simply not acceptable to anglophones as a place to build a life. And the proof of this is vividly evident in the continuing departure of English Quebecers, especially the young.

There are quite a few anglophones in Quebec who are bitter about the way the language debate has turned out. I don't agree with them. Many promises were made by the Liberal Party and not kept. But it's not unusual for political parties to neglect the solemn engagements in their party program when they find themselves in power. The debate was conducted in a very open way; everyone had a chance to express their point of view. Bill 101 and its amendments have been adopted democratically and, for the most part, within the framework of Quebec's constitutional powers. What has happened, put simply, is that Quebec's francophone majority has given absolute priority to its own "aspirations." There's nothing a minority as small as the English community in Quebec can do about this.

There is no point in feeling bitter about coming second in a political debate. There is a point in seeking to understand what happened, and in using this understanding as a guide for action.

6

The Two Founding Nations

I hope I've convinced you that Quebec's political behaviour over the past twenty years has been somewhat ethnocentric. However, most Canadians have never lived in Quebec and don't intend to. They have not been exposed to the daily assault on the emotions, which arrives each morning with the Montreal *Gazette*, or to the excitement of a referendum campaign. English Canadians in Nova Scotia or British Columbia might argue "Why not let them do what they want in Quebec? There's no reason for them to separate. We wouldn't want to live there but what they do in Montreal doesn't affect us here in Truro."

But it does. Quebec's politics have had a profound effect on the politics of the rest of the country. Quebec's domestic policies have a direct impact on the character of its membership in the Canadian federation. This connection is most clearly illustrated in the continuing debate on whether that province should be given a "special status" in the Canadian federation.

Can a nation-state find peace within a federal constitution? Attempts to resolve the inherent contradictions have provided steady jobs for hundreds of constitutional lawyers, university professors, and newspaper columnists for over a century. They haven't succeeded, but even today you can find people who believe it can be done. I am one of those who has tried.

My experience with the beast began in Ottawa, in 1977. The victory of René Lévesque's separatist government in Quebec inspired Prime Minister Trudeau to create a royal commission to manage the consequences of this event. Jean-Luc Pépin was appointed co-chairman of the Task Force on Canadian Unity (which became popularly known as the Pépin-Robarts Commission), and that cheerful and intelligent soldier in the service of good causes asked me to be its executive director.

The task force was originally conceived by the Prime Minister's Office to coordinate the activities of numerous patriotic groups that sprang up across the country in response to the separatist victory in 1976. Today we only dimly remember the National Survival Institute, Decision-Canada, Commitment-Canada, Ralli-Canada, Quebec-Canada, Participation-Quebec, Positive Action, Unity Train, Westerners for Canadian Unity, Destiny-Canada, Committee for an Independent Canada, and Canada-United. But at the time these organizations were being created at the rate of one a week and they all wanted to *do something*. The Pépin-Robarts Commission was invented to help them find a practical vocation. That, at least, was the way Pierre Trudeau saw it.

But Jean-Luc Pépin had a better idea. He wanted to rewrite the Constitution. And in a series of adroit moves that would justify a separate book, and over the strenuous objections of the Prime Minister, he succeeded in getting the Commission's mandate changed to enable him to do just that.

I was the general manager of the project and it would have been a lot easier to supervise the Metropolitan Opera. It seemed that everyone wanted to save the country. We rounded up a group of commissioners, staff members, and advisors that resembled a galaxy of shooting stars, and the discord and confusion in the country was faithfully reflected within our walls. Yet, thanks to some inspired work, brilliantly synthesized by the Commission's research director, David Cameron, its final report became the first serious response by Canada to the contemporary separatist movement.[1] Some people consider it's still the best one.

Many subjects were addressed in the report. But the key objective – the reason for the task force's existence – was to persuade Quebecers to vote for Canada.

The solution it came up with was based on a recurring theme in Canada's political history: the Pépin-Robarts report proposed that we explicitly recognize the "duality" of our country in the Constitution.

The ancestry of this idea can be traced back through about eight generations of Canadians. As it is central to an understanding of our existential problem, a brief digression to explain it is required.

The issue is whether or not Canada is composed of "Two Founding Nations." Some historians claim this expression was invented by Honoré Mercier in the Quebec election campaign of 1887,[2] but the idea goes back further than that, to a hypothesis about how the country was created. It's the notion that "Canada" is the name of a contract between the English and the French – and that the country cannot even exist unless Quebec is a part of it.

The Two Nations theory can best be understood by looking at the positions of those who take it very seriously – and those who think it's a bad joke.

Those who subscribe to the theory hold that Canada's original Constitution, the British North America Act, was a pact, a contract between two equal nations. Therefore, any important changes should only be made with the consent of both parties.

The nations in question are the French from France, represented at the time of Confederation by the leaders of the colony
that had once been known as Lower Canada, and the English
from Great Britain who were living mainly in Upper Canada. It
is held that the contract they made is still binding on us all, and
that its rights and responsibilities have been inherited by
Quebec on the one hand, and by the rest of Canada (or perhaps
Ottawa) on the other.

In its most extreme form the theory holds that the central
government of Canada was created by these two nations, which
therefore continue to have the permanent right to define what
Ottawa may and may not do.

The opposing viewpoint, held by some very respectable historians, is that Confederation had nothing to do with a pact
between two nations, and very little to do with language issues.
They point out that the Confederation project involved four
provinces, not two. Nova Scotia and New Brunswick, as well as
Ontario and Quebec, were part of the original deal. Prince
Edward Island and Newfoundland were also involved in the
negotiations.

More important, they argue that the agreement in question
was not a contract but an Act of the British Parliament, drafted
and adopted in London. This Act makes no mention, anywhere,
of two founding nations or of any special status accorded to a
member of the new federation. The issues of Quebec's autonomy were fully debated in Quebec at the time of Confederation,
notably by Cartier, Langevin, and Dorion,[3] and settled, with the
approval of the Quebec Legislature, by an acceptable allocation
of powers to the provinces within the new federal system.

The Act does contain a number of concessions to linguistic,
religious, and other interest groups. In this respect it's just like
any other piece of legislation. But if the document had been

intended to incarnate the principle of the equality of two founding nations it could have said so explicitly, and it didn't.

According to this view, the federation was an administrative rearrangement of the British colonies in North America, designed to strengthen them against possible American invasion and create a stronger base for expansion to the west, while preserving local autonomy. These objectives were supported as strongly by the colonists, French and English, as they were by the imperial power. In the words of Cartier, Confederation was "necessary for our commercial interests, prosperity and efficient defence."[4] With this overriding purpose, peripheral issues, language and cultural matters, along with a number of other local preoccupations, are addressed in the details of the legislative text. "Read it," say the critics. "There is no more there than meets the eye."

Now these two views, though diametrically opposed, have the great advantage of clarity. But very few Canadians would agree completely with either of them. French Quebecers, generally speaking, cling to the idea that there was a pact, admittedly not one which was written into the Constitution, but which can nonetheless be demonstrated by events and declarations in the years leading up to Confederation.

More pertinently, they feel they were discriminated against as the country expanded after Confederation. As a result of this expansion, Canada now consists not of four provinces but ten, and nine of them are predominately English speaking. That's a fact and it's not going to change. So most Quebecers reluctantly accept that the implementation of meaningful policies based on the concept of two founding nations, coast to coast, has now become impossible.

The urge to find something to replace it did not arise last week. It is founded in a belief that Quebec is the "*foyer*" of the

French nation in Canada and that, if francophones cannot share the full Canadian space equally with the English then they will, at least, be indisputably in control within Quebec. Constructed on two centuries of nationalism, the concept has been expressed in recent years as "autonomy" (Jean Lesage), "Equality or Independence" (Daniel Johnson, Sr.), and "cultural sovereignty" (Robert Bourassa). A number of texts have been devised to reflect this vision in the Constitution – the Fulton-Favreau Formula, the Victoria Declaration, the Meech Lake Accord, the Charlottetown Accord – but none has been acceptable to all parties.

It is argued that the right of the Quebec Legislature to control everything required to ensure the continuing Frenchness of its residents must now be formally acknowledged and accepted by the rest of Canada. Federalist French Quebecers have baptized this concept with the name of "special status," to be made manifest by the recognition of Quebec as a distinct (or unique) society. They suggest that the unity crisis can be resolved once and for all by adding such an expression of Quebec's distinctiveness at some appropriate place in the Constitution.

There is no consensus on what this might mean in practice. Some argue that a symbolic gesture is sufficient. Others believe the amendment should give Quebec full authority to choose the powers it wishes to exercise and the ones it wishes to leave with the federal government in Ottawa. There are also a number of intermediate proposals.

Most people who oppose special status for Quebec argue that Canada is, after all, a federation, and the provincial powers with which Quebec is presently equipped – in language and culture, education, social security and economic affairs – already enable it to express its distinctiveness in a very convincing way. But the different proposals for special status are all based on a single idea: that Quebec needs to become more profoundly, more completely French than it is today, or than it can ever be with the existing division of powers.

Within francophone Quebec, for everyone who is not a separatist, the formal recognition of Quebec as a distinct society is the minimum condition for ending the constitutional debate and accepting life within the Canadian family. In every Quebec election, all parties have this proposal, or something even more radical, in their program.

It seems like a simple remedy to cure such a persistent malaise. However, it's too good to be true. In order for it to work its magic, precise words must be found, and located in the Constitution in a way that will make Quebecers believe that they are really getting special powers – and make the rest of the country believe that they aren't.

Since the election of the Parti Québécois in 1976, a number of commissions have wrestled with the problem. Most of them have sought a way out of the conundrum by proposing a formulation that is deliberately vague, leaving the Supreme Court to decide what "special status" or "distinct society" might mean in practice.

Pépin-Robarts came up with its own version of a solution. It proposed that we recognize, in a preamble to the Constitution, "the historic partnership between English and French-speaking Canadians, and the distinctiveness of Quebec."[5] In the case of culture, this general declaration was to be made specific by giving Quebec "an essential role and responsibility for the preservation and strengthening of the French heritage in its own territory."[6] This declaration of intent would be turned over to the courts, which would let us know, in their interpretations over time, exactly what this "French heritage" was all about.

It was presumed that this proposal would go over very nicely in Quebec. But what about the rest of the country, which was opposed to special recognition for one province?

The answer was simplicity itself. Pépin-Robarts proposed that we make a promise in the Constitution to "recognize the distinctive status *of any province*"[7] (my emphasis) that wanted to fill out an application form.

This was not, to put it mildly, an exact translation of the theory of the two founding nations. In retrospect it sounds fantastic.

In any event, the whole report was disowned as a sell-out to the separatists by the Trudeau government which had commissioned it. However, in Quebec it was well received by the federalists, who saw it as an attractive alternative to independence for the referendum debate that was to be held a few months later.

At the time, the leader of the federalist forces in Quebec was Claude Ryan. He was in the process of concocting his own proposals for constitutional reform. I had an opportunity to participate in his project as well, because in June 1978 I left the Pépin-Robarts Task Force and became a Liberal member of the Quebec National Assembly.

Ryan's constitutional reform proposals were clear. Their purpose was to "affirm the fundamental equality of the two founding peoples who have given, and still provide, this country its unique place in the family of nations. This basic dualism must be consecrated in the supreme document of the country."[8] To permit this affirmation, it was proposed that Quebec be given "guarantees capable of facilitating the protection and the affirmation of its distinct personality."[9]

Twenty years later, Ryan's idea remains, essentially unchanged, as the policy of the Quebec Liberal Party.[10] Its proposal of constitutionally based duality is the only alternative to separatism on offer in Quebec's political life. These options have not sprung untested from the policy committees of Quebec's two political parties. They are the only two that find support among francophone voters. There is virtually no support in francophone Quebec for the existing federal system.

So there is a connection between Quebec's efforts to remake its own political space in the image of the French language and culture, and the political life of the country as a whole. The home of the French "founding nation," if it is to remain with us, must be given constitutional powers that the other provinces do not have, to enable it to realize its *projet de société.*" And other Canadians, whether they be of British, Chinese, or Italian origin, must accept that this one language and culture – and one only – has a "special status" in our federation.

What additional powers will flow from this special status? No one can say because no one in Quebec is interested in defining exactly what special status means, what precise new powers are involved, and how finality may be achieved. There is no consensus on this in Quebec because the benefit for Quebecers is not to be found in an answer to the question. It lies in the negotiating process itself, the use of the concept of special status to unceasingly enlarge the political powers of the Quebec government over its citizens, and reduce those of Ottawa. There can be no angle of repose.

Quebec: A Nation-State

We have seen that all Quebec governments, with the massive approval of the francophone population, have given themselves the overriding political mission to strengthen and expand the French language and culture. And they are accomplishing this by restricting the development of other languages and cultures, notably English. They have been doing this quite effectively with their existing powers. But Quebecers are nearly unanimous in a conviction that they have not gone far enough, and that the Canadian Constitution requires serious adjustment in order to complete the project.

Some Canadians persist in believing that these are the views only of the separatists, that most Quebecers don't take these issues seriously and really want to "get on with their lives" in the same way as the rest of us. This is not the case, and the prevailing sentiment is faithfully reflected in the policies of the only two parties that could possibly win an election. A Quebecer who believes the Canadian Constitution to be acceptable as it is, or who refuses to be concerned with its imperfections, might just as well not bother to vote.

It is interesting to note how this polarization came about. In 1976, after the election that brought the Parti Québécois to power, there were three other parties with seats in the Quebec National Assembly: the Liberals, the Union Nationale, and the Social Credit Party. However, the pressure on all members of the National Assembly to declare themselves for or against separatism put an end to these alternatives. Between 1977 and 1980 every member of the Union Nationale and Social Credit parties defected to either the Parti Québécois or the Liberals, and the two smaller parties were disbanded. They have not been heard from since.

Over the past twenty years, a number of efforts have been made to create alternative parties in Quebec, but, due to fear of splitting the vote on the independence issue, none has enjoyed more than momentary success. The Parti Québécois and the Liberals remain the only political alternatives, each with slightly different answers to the National Question, but indistinguishable on every other issue of public policy. Since 1980, political debate as it is known in the rest of Canada, the United States, and Europe, has ceased to exist in Quebec.

The only two parties in Quebec have a common political ideology and govern in essentially the same way. Life is the same regardless of which one is in power. Their agreement on the priority that should be given to francophone affirmation is nuanced only by a difference of opinion on the constitutional base from which this unending process is to be launched. For one, it is independence with association; for the other, a new and privileged position within the existing Canadian Constitution.

The ideology of both parties is grounded in ethnic and linguistic nationalism. The views of the Parti Québécois are well known. The Liberal Party too has a very specific position on this issue. Its basic policy document begins with an appeal to the Quebec people to find a "new definition" for themselves, based on a certain number of shared values.[1] "Foremost" among the shared values it identifies is not human rights, or compassion, or even liberty, but "the French language and the rich cultural heritage it embodies."[2]

The Liberals are just as insistent as their adversaries in arguing that the present federal system is unacceptable. In an expression which defies translation they argue that the only doorway to harmonious relations with the rest of Canada is formal recognition of "*les revendications traditionnelles du Québec profond.*" They promise to keep Quebec in Canada, provided the role of the federal government is drastically reduced and Quebec is given additional powers to reinforce its "shared values." Their current position is that "currency and the banking system, foreign policy, the defence of the country, the control of the borders, telecommunications, and interprovincial transportation"[3] should be the powers retained by the Canadian government. That's as far as current public opinion will allow a Quebec political party to go in its vision of a role for the Canadian federation.

As for special status, they insist that "as long as Canada has not recognized in a more explicit manner the distinct character of Quebec, the balance which it defines will remain subject to debate not only by sovereignists but also by many Quebec federalists. The present situation generates tension and uncertainty."[4]

The only francophone organization in Quebec which argues that the federal system doesn't need to be reinvented is a movement, Cité Libre. A few hundred in number, its members publish an interesting journal and meet every month in a Chinese restaurant to deplore the nationalist tendencies of their brethren. Devout separatists consider them to be traitors. Other Quebecers find them eccentric. There is not a single elected politician in Quebec, federal or provincial, who endorses their position.

In a province where separatists form the government, and support for the existing federal system is confined to a movement, one might think that the die was already cast. But it's not that simple. When it comes to action the population maintains a state of ambivalence, which is reflected in a corresponding ambiguity among the political classes. If the polls suggest that a spirit of conciliation is in the air, the separatists speak fondly of their proposed association with Canada. If the population gets irritable with Ottawa, the Liberals talk tough. So it's not surprising that each party attracts about half the vote. The two parties alternate in power, depending mainly on the popularity of their leader at any given moment.

As for Quebec's representation in Ottawa, a comparable situation exists. To ensure attention and respect for their priorities, Quebec voters send a substantial number of members of Parliament to Ottawa from both the separatist and federalist parties. At the time of writing the count was federalists 30 seats, separatists 45 seats. In the 1997 federal election the separatist party received about half of the francophone vote in Quebec; Liberals and Conservatives divided the other half about equally. The separatist members of Parliament go to Ottawa with the sole mission of arguing that they should not be there. They make no other contribution to the public life of our country. Quebec's political analysts say the people of Quebec are sending a message to the rest of the country. It's hard to disagree.

Keeping these two choices alive is comforting to Quebecers, and there is no indication that the situation is going to change. From a Quebec standpoint there is no reason why it should. The threat of separation, omnipresent but never carried out, has guaranteed the province a degree of attention at all levels of Canadian public-policy making that serves it very well. In Quebec itself, the English have been almost completely excluded from public life. But Ottawa is bilingual, and Ottawa stays focused on Quebec's interests. Every political decision taken in the national capital, be it a political nomination, a subsidy, or a new law, is considered in light of whether it will help or hinder the cause of the separatists in Quebec. An informal quota system creates many interesting job opportunities for Quebec's political and economic elite in Ottawa, and in Quebec itself, where a vast array of federal institutions provide employment and contracts for services of all kinds. The reaction in the rest of the country is predictable, and understandable.

Instinctively, francophone Quebecers are aware that the present situation provides them with the best of all possible worlds. They have no practical reason to vote for a party that proposes that Quebec is a province *comme les autres*, to separate, or to put an end to the separatist movement. In the national-unity debate the idealists are to be found in the rest of Canada. Quebecers are pragmatists.

One clear indication of this mindset can be found in the business community. While most of Quebec's business leaders are opposed to independence, they almost unanimously support the demand for special status. Marcel Côté, president of a major consulting firm, is perhaps the most outspoken member of Quebec's business elite in his opposition to separation. He is a personal friend and I know that he would object strenuously to being considered a nationalist. And yet, in his recent book *Le Rêve de la terre promise*, which is a vivid analysis of the costs of separation, he argues that the only alternative is "the recognition of our national identity, as a people, defined essentially by a language, and a territory, Quebec. Collectively, we are the masters of our own political destiny and we can choose the structures that we desire. Our political voice is principally, and first of all, the government of Quebec."[5] It's worth repeating that Quebec's business leaders don't get any more federalist than Marcel Côté.

Not one person among the francophone elite – among the board members of Canada's largest corporations, the academic community, the editorial writers – has ever argued that Quebec should bring the unity debate to an end by accepting the Canadian Constitution as it is written today. There is nothing for them to gain by doing so, and much to lose. The columnist Lysiane Gagnon has summed it up thus: "It is socially acceptable for a francophone Quebecer to be a federalist, but he will have to justify himself each time the subject comes up in a conversation with friends or family. . . . What he must never say is 1) that the status quo is acceptable; 2) that he loves Canada."[6]

An interesting summary of the cultivated ambiguity of Quebecers on the constitutional issue is provided in a recent book by three distinguished political scientists. In *Un Combat inachevé*, Maurice Pinard, Robert Bernier, and Vincent Lemieux review a vast array of polls that have been taken in Quebec on the constitutional issue and on Quebecers' attitudes to Canada, some going back as far as 1960.[7]

One is immediately struck by the complexity of the questions that the pollsters have invented. Quebecers are a people seeking their destiny armed only with a dictionary. They are constantly being asked whether they are in favour of "sovereignty," "independence," "separation," "sovereignty-association," "special status," "renewed federalism," or the "status quo." None of these expressions comes with a definition attached – they are political battle cries – so respondents are obliged to reply to the pollsters on the basis of their affection for the last politician who used the expression on the TV news.

Polls on any given subject, prepared for organizations with different agendas, produce quite different results. For example, a survey conducted for the Council for Canadian Unity in April 1998 disclosed that 63 percent of all Quebecers believe that "Canadian federalism can satisfy both Quebec and Canada."[8] It was followed two months later by a poll for the separatist newspaper *Le Devoir*, which revealed that only 37 percent of all Quebecers believe it is possible to "reform Canadian federalism in a way which will satisfy both Quebec and the rest of Canada."[9]

The benefit of the book by Pinard, Bernier, and Lemieux is that it examines a vast number of polls taken over a long period, which permits us to understand the underlying tendencies:

- Only about 10 percent of francophone voters are in favour of the Canadian Constitution as it is.
- About 10 percent of the total Quebec population is in favour of unconditional independence, about 30 percent want "sovereignty," and the "Yes" vote can get up to around 50 percent if it is clearly attached to a promise of an economic association with Canada.
- About 20 percent of those in favour of sovereignty-association are confused about what it means. They believe, for instance, that Quebec would still be a Canadian province.
- About 25 percent of those who would vote "Yes" would do so for strategic reasons, to increase Quebec's bargaining power. (On the other hand, 30 percent of the francophones who voted "No" to independence in the 1995 referendum say that they are in favour of sovereignty-association!)[10]

These figures appear to be stable over time, although they may rise or fall temporarily in response to political initiatives and catastrophes, and the personal popularity of the party leaders.

In Quebec the process of francophone affirmation is stated in positive terms. But it has a negative side. It is based on a struggle for a limited space. So, if the linguistic and ethnic goals of Quebec are to be realized, then the English, both in Quebec and in the rest of Canada, must be portrayed as the enemy. The maintenance of tension between the two language groups is essential. The call to remain eternally vigilant against the encroachment of the English – their strength, our weakness – provides the vital energy for ethnic nationalism. And, inevitably, English becomes not only a language but also a place. If the identity of Quebecers is to be found in their language, then by definition they must be discouraged from developing a Canadian identity because the language associated with that identity is, and will remain, English. In making French the cause, and English the enemy, the people of francophone Canada have gone to war with their fellow citizens.

The book by Pinard, Bernier, and Lemieux illustrates the results of this policy. The percentage of Quebec francophones who identify themselves primarily as Canadians has dropped from 34 percent in 1970 to 9 percent in 1990.[11] A full quarter of the population says it now feels no attachment whatsoever to Canada.

However, it should also be pointed out that about 60 percent of Quebec's francophones do feel some attachment to the country as a whole and Pinard devotes the better part of a chapter to an analysis of this group. What emerges is the conclusion that about one-half of these people (29 percent of the francophone population) are attached to Canada essentially for its economic benefits: "only because it provides me with a high standard of living."[12]

This means that 70 percent of all francophone Quebecers want either to break all ties with Canada or remain associated with it for one reason only – economic security. The referendum debate of 1995 was grounded in this premise. Those who opposed independence, led by the Liberals, spent no time expounding the virtues of membership in a community of Canadians. They simply produced a dozen or so studies to prove that separation would be an economic disaster. Those who supported independence concentrated on the same issue. They said, "Not to worry – we guarantee you a continuing economic association with Canada just like the one you have now. No jobs will be lost."

This is the francophone political consensus. It's not really an opinion. It's an instinct, made manifest in two political parties with one destination, and in two different propositions for getting there.

The leaders of both Quebec parties contend that if their current demands for reform are met, be it sovereignty-association or distinct society, then the relationship between Quebec and Canada will be stabilized once and for all. Some English Canadians also believe this, in a slightly different way. They imagine that the people of Quebec are being led astray by a gang of fanatics, and that, if the federalists would only get their act together, Quebecers would throw them out and become good Canadians again.

There are also people who believe in fairies and there is no way of proving them wrong. But the idea that eternal harmony between Quebec and the rest of Canada can be created by the magic bullet of a constitutional amendment flies in the face of history – and reality.

Nationalism is not a single isolated idea. It can best be understood as one element on the edge of a rainbow of ideas, concrete objectives, and fantasies, each one fading seamlessly into the next. To get rid of separatism, it would be necessary to get rid of the whole rainbow, one which has been inspiring the Quebec francophone community for two centuries. It would be necessary to locate and elect a political leader who would take the organization of Quebec's national holiday away from the Société

St-Jean-Baptiste, put *"La Belle Province"* back on the licence plates, and then drive to Ottawa and put Quebec's signature on the Canadian Constitution. At the time of writing no one has applied for this job. It is my belief that no one ever will.

On Moral Bonds

I think it's time to ask Quebec to leave the federation, for a single reason: because the political values of that province are fundamentally and permanently incompatible with those of the rest of the country. But what are the political values of the rest of the country? This is a book about Canada and it's time to take a closer look at what we'll have left when the process of Divestiture is completed.

What is the Rest of Canada?

Quebecers know who they are. It seems clear to all Quebecers that their province has a distinct identity and, they like to add mischievously, that the Rest of Canada has no identity at all. Lucien Bouchard, the premier of Quebec, once declared that, in his opinion, the Rest of Canada wasn't even a country. The Rest of Us have not exactly contradicted him. We have tortured ourselves for the past hundred years with the question *Who are we?*

The first problem is to figure out what we are we going to call ourselves. Canada without Quebec does not have a name. Philip Resnick, in a recent book,[1] called it "English Canada," but the adjective is superfluous. The nine provinces and the territories cannot be understood with reference to the languages spoken by the people who live there. Most of them are certainly going to be using English, but that's not a defining feature of the place. We wouldn't call it "Democratic Canada" or "Cold Canada," either. These facts of life don't have to appear on our birth certificate. The rest of Canada is simply Canada. But to indicate that it's not the same country we have today, I'll be referring to it within these pages in italics, as *Canada*.

French Quebecers, with few exceptions, will not object to our use of this name. For the past twenty years the existential debate in their province has been played out as "Quebec v. *Canada*." Their own affinity for our country is now measured mainly in terms of the economic benefits it provides. Even federalist Quebecers are Quebecers first. They seem prepared to let us have this internationally respected trademark, so let's use it.

Our country of nine (and someday perhaps more) provinces will still be recognized as *Canada* everywhere in the world: at the UN, NATO, and the Olympic Games. It will have at least 22 million citizens. In terms of GDP it will still be one of the most important countries in the world (in twelfth place, ahead of the Russian Federation), and its GDP per capita will put it in the top ten.[2]

The statistics are readily accessible. We also know where the national boundaries are. But nobody seems to have ever come up with a pleasing definition of the *Canadian* identity.

It hasn't been for lack of trying, which in itself is a bit peculiar. People in other parts of the world seem to know who they are – even who we are. But, inside our country, there's a strong feeling that something is missing, that we need a *Canadian* mission statement, a job description. Exactly how its existence could make us happier or richer is not clear. But, even though many books and articles have been written in an attempt to satisfy this demand, the uncertainty persists. So, like many before us, we're now going to go in search of the *Canadian* identity.

I'd like to keep the project to a manageable size, and resist the tendency to get politics mixed up with life. Being *Canadian* is just one of the things we do; we find delight in many smaller solidarities. We are also Newfoundlanders, Methodists, Torontonians, workers, first-generation Chinese, computer freaks, hockey fans – and so on. We are family, participants in the fellowship of the breadbox. Above all, we are ourselves: each of us the embodiment of hopes and fears that we have to deal with alone, as individuals.

I would argue that there's only one thing that all *Canadians* have in common: it's our Constitution. *Canada* is just a political system. And in the words of Michael Oakeshott, "Politics is not concerned with anything or everything which may come into a man's head to want and to contend for, but with the consideration of the arrangements and rules which give shape to an association of human beings."

Canada is such an association of human beings, united only in the rules of their common residence. These "rules" are to be found in the Canadian Constitution: our two orders of government, the allocation of powers between them, a Charter of Rights and Freedoms, a judiciary. It is in these institutions, their evolution, and the values which underlie them, that we must seek our identity as *Canadians*.

However, for most *Canadians* this definition of our country will not be sufficient. We will insist that there is more to our national identity than the words in our Constitution. We want to recognize ourselves in a set of common values that guide our political leaders in their conduct of public policy. We feel that we share some kind of moral bond with other *Canadians*. I believe that there is one, but our search for it must follow a very narrow path between two contemporary political ideologies that are both powerful and irreconcilable. To understand them we must venture for the next few pages into the world of political theory.

One of these ideologies is a school of thought very much in style these days, which holds that the state has no role to play in defining any kind of public morality for its citizens. It's a central theme in the public-policy debate in the United States and has been given a worldwide boost by the Cold War victory of the market economy over the forces of social and economic planning. Those who embrace this ideology believe that the role of government is to provide its citizens with as much freedom as possible to pursue their personal goals – and that's all. No unifying ethic should be defined or imposed. They call this the "procedural" society.

On the other side of our path lie a number of ideologies which insist that governments have a responsibility to define the good life for everyone, and govern in a way which is consistent with that vision. Some of these ideologies – social democracy, for instance – can be advocated, pursued, abandoned, and reinvented within the framework of a liberal Constitution. But one of them, nationalism, requires that the state itself, and its Constitution, be structured for the achievement of these collective purposes. Nationalism proposes that the state should be designed around the values of one specific language, religious, or ethnic group. The idea is very much alive today. Spectacular examples can be found in the Balkans and the Middle East, and a more modest specimen is close at hand, in the province of Quebec.

Canada is neither a procedural society nor a nation-state. The moral bond that unites us lies between these two extremes.

We're Not a "Procedural" Society

A good description of the procedural society can be found in a recent book by Michael J. Sandel entitled *Democracy's Discontent.*[3] An accessible summary appeared in the *Atlantic Monthly* of March 1996.[4] Sandel points out that a procedural society is based on the premise that politics should not try to "legislate morality." Proceduralists insist that "government should not affirm, through its policies or laws, any particular conception of the good life; instead it should provide a neutral framework of rights within which people can choose their own values and ends."

Sandel opposes this vision of public life and argues that it contains the seeds of its own downfall. He points out that the procedural state "cannot secure the liberty it promises, because it cannot inspire the sense of community and civic engagement that liberty requires." He believes there is no way to secure freedom without attending to the character of citizens and points out that individual liberty can't exist outside the legal framework of a community. The capitalist requires it, for a generally accepted definition of, and protection of, private property. Artists need it, to provide some community-based rules that ensure freedom of expression.

Sandel argues that both liberals and conservatives invoke the virtues of the "value-free" state, but only when it suits their purpose: liberals, when faced with laws that mandate school prayers or limit abortions; conservatives, when confronted with the issues of environmental protection or distributive justice. A dazzling example of these contradictions can be found in some advice given recently by the Reverend Jesse Jackson to the United States Supreme Court: "To ignore race and gender is racist and sexist."

Sandel believes that the very existence of a state implies that the people within it are together because they share some common purpose, seek some common good, and that by sharing in self-rule they are acknowledging a moral bond with their community. In consequence he argues for a "republican" society, one in which all citizens possess, or come to acquire, certain civic virtues. He says that "the republican conception of freedom requires a formative politics, a politics that cultivates in citizens the qualities of character that self-government requires."

Sandel admits that there are enormous difficulties facing anyone who tries to define and teach the values of a particular state. Given the increasing diversity of people grouped together within national boundaries, how can we establish a lasting consensus on the moral code that should apply to all? This may have been simple in Aristotle's *polis* or the agrarian colonies of Thomas Jefferson. Today it is bound to be spectacularly controversial.

But in another sense this complexity makes a definition of the role of the citizen and the state even more necessary. Faced with the difficulties of modern life, it is not only the weak who turn to their government. We are not rootless, atomistic individuals floating free of any ties to society. Even the most devout libertarians are likely at some point to feel overwhelmed as they face the world with only their personal resources. The fact that the state exists implies that it has a "reason." And in the case of a modern state – of *Canada* – with its increasing influence on the private lives of a widely dispersed and varied people, such an answer must invoke a moral justification that is understood and accepted by all members of our community.

WE'RE NOT A "NATION-STATE"

On the other hand, moral bonds have to be handled with care. It's hard to find one with which everybody can agree. And history provides eloquent reminders that when the "bond" is defined so as to benefit only part of the community – the majority, or perhaps a minority which controls the police force – all kinds of abuses can be committed in the name of "national affirmation."

There is an idea going the rounds these days that the end of the Cold War has left people feeling insecure, deprived of the labels and the identity that comforted them when they were obliged to live in the "East" or the "West." This void has been aggravated by "globalization," a phenomenon that seems to diminish people's ability to control their own destiny. So, the argument goes, we are turning back to our roots and seeking reassurance in ethnic nationalism by creating new states based on common racial, religious, or linguistic origins. A dozen or more books have been written recently to make this point. Among them is Michael Ignatieff's *Blood and Belonging*.[5] The ethnic states he illustrates are Croatia and Serbia, Germany, Ukraine, Kurdistan, Northern Ireland – and Quebec.

It's not clear whether this way of seeing the world is the reflection of real change in our behaviour patterns or just an academic fashion. But there is no doubt that long before the Berlin Wall came down, nationalism was a potent force in the world order. I made its acquaintance for the first time, not in the corridors of Quebec's National Assembly, but a few years earlier, at the London School of Economics.

In a weekly seminar called "The History of Political Thought" I was introduced to the history and the power of nationalism by Michael Oakeshott, Elie Kedourie, Ken Minogue, and Bill Letwin. They had all written on the subject. They all understood it – and disliked it. And their reasoning was constructed on an impressive foundation of scholarship and articulated with great elegance. Their arguments made sense to me then and, after spending twenty years testing them against the realities of political life in Quebec and *Canada*, they still do.

The words "nation" and "nationalism" have been given many meanings and there is an enormous literature on the subject. But a common thread is the proposition that a state, a country, should be composed of people of a single race, or religious belief or language or culture, and preferably with more than one of these features in common. In the words of Minogue, the nation-state is based on a concept of "pre-political unity." The idea here is that a country made up entirely of Jews, or of white Anglo-Saxon Protestants, will be easier to manage, and more pleasant for its inhabitants to live in, than one which encompasses people of many races, languages and religions. Professor Kedourie's description of nationalism is a "doctrine that holds that humanity is naturally divided into nations, that nations are known by certain characteristics which can be ascertained and that the only legitimate type of government is national self-government."[6]

Nationalism is a relatively recent invention, unknown until the beginning of the eighteenth century. It was given a mighty boost by the American President, Woodrow Wilson, in the months after the First World War, when in order to dispose of the remnants of the Hapsburg Empire, he invented the term "self-determination" and established it as a guiding principle of international law. The United States senator Daniel Moynihan has described the consequences of Wilson's declaration for the people of Europe, the Middle East, and Africa in his book *Pandaemonium: Ethnicity in International Politics*. They are not very pretty. Moynihan notes that "the world quickly discovered that minorities not infrequently seek self-determination for themselves in order to deny it to others."[7] Wilson did not live to face the consequences of his grand idea. But America has spent the past seventy years trying to figure out which of the world's governments, born in the cradle of "self-determination," should be given diplomatic recognition, and when – and for how long.

To be fair to the smaller nations of the world it should be pointed out that the chaos and suffering consequent on nationalism have not been confined to the Balkans and sub-Saharan Africa. The great nation-states of Europe learned nothing from the First World War. Twenty years later they provided us with a second one.

Kedourie and Minogue were preoccupied with the consequences of nationalism and they were not impressed. Kedourie summed it up like this: "The attempt to fashion so much of the world on national lines has not led to greater peace and stability. On the contrary, it has created new conflicts, exacerbated tensions and brought catastrophe to numberless people innocent of all politics."[8]

Oakeshott was less interested in the consequences of nationalism than in how it arises and in the kind of person who espouses it. For him the nationalist is the "individual *manqué*," a person suffering from some "combination of actual loss, debility, ignorance, timidity, poverty, loneliness, displacement, persecution or misfortune." These people can be identified by "their inability to sustain an individual life and their longing for the shelter of a community." For him, the nation-state could best be understood as "an association of invalids, all victims of the same disease and incorporated in seeking relief from their common ailment."[9] For Oakeshott, it was one thing to have a sense of place, and quite another to be obsessed with it.

Not everyone, of course, sees nationalism so darkly. For instance, socialists, who believe that the state should define and pursue an "ideal" society for everyone, tend to be sympathetic to nationalism, which has a similar vision, albeit for a more restricted clientele. One of these is Charles Taylor, the distinguished Canadian philosopher, who has been a prominent apologist for the nationalist cause in recent years. His views are particularly interesting because he is an English-speaking Quebecer who appears to be specifically advancing the cause of francophone nationalism in his own province.

In a number of essays and addresses, Taylor has argued that protecting and improving the French language and culture in Quebec is akin to protecting and improving the environment and, for this reason, the majority has the right to impose the appropriate conditions on all of the population. He traces the evolution of this line of reasoning back to Johann Gottfried van Herder and the German Romantics who followed him, and applies it to life in Quebec. The reasoning is elaborate but a few quotes will give the flavour of the argument as it applies to his province: "It is axiomatic for Quebec governments that the survival and flourishing of French culture is a good. . . . It involves making sure that there is a community of people here in the future that will want to avail itself of the opportunity to use the French language. . . . They are willing to weigh the importance of certain forms of uniform treatment against the importance of cultural survival and opt sometimes in favor of the latter. . . . Obviously, I would endorse this kind of model."[10]

Such is Taylor's justification for Quebec nationalism. When asked, he agrees that this right to political recognition would apply, in principle, equally to the anglophone partitionist movement in Quebec, and to Canada's native people. Faced with potentially unlimited demands for this kind of endorsement Taylor has suggested that different "levels of diversity" might be recognized.[11] He argues that a person of Ukrainian extraction might settle for political recognition simply as one piece in the Canadian mosaic, while accepting that a more extended recognition, of a "second level or 'deep' diversity," is appropriate for the French and the Inuit. The best one can say of such a policy is that it presents a political and administrative challenge. In practice it runs the serious risk of giving us a country structured in response to the demands of the largest, wealthiest, and best-organized ethnic groups.

In any event, Taylor has come up with arguments which explain the nation-state, and has demonstrated that Quebec fits the description. He believes that "a society can be organized around a definition of the good life, without this being seen as a deprecation of those who do not personally share this definition."[12] He maintains that Quebec is justified in defining itself in this way. And Taylor may be right about this. The Quebec idea, even if you don't agree with it, is at least an idea. And like it or not, Taylor's description of Quebec rings true. If nationalism can be identified by a feeling of "pre-political unity," by "characteristics which can be ascertained in advance," then the government of the province of Quebec is certainly the government of a nation-state, defined by one language, one culture. This theme is the touchstone of its political vision, and defines or colours all its political actions. I think no one disputes this any more.

However, this description cannot be applied to *Canada*. *Canada* is not like Quebec. It's another kind of country. Taylor's arguments don't help us to understand the moral code that unites *Canadians*. *Canada* is not a procedural society. But neither is it a nation-state, whether we propose to define it in terms of one nation, or two, or three. There is no pre-political unity, no race or language group or culture that is generally seen as worthy of special status in *Canada*, except, for very special reasons, the native people.

How do we find our way down the path between the excesses of the procedural state and the nation-state? What is the moral good that defines the *Canadian* community and gives it a meaning with which we are all comfortable? Some refer to it as a "civil society." But because *Canada* encompasses many "societies" – in the generally accepted sense of that term – we'll use Oakeshott's expression and call it a "civil association."

Canada: In Prose

I'm aware that many *Canadians* are going to feel that "civil association," as the cornerstone of our national identity, is pretty thin gruel for the nourishment of national loyalty and pride. It sounds like something a lawyer dreamed up. Surely there's a way to be a little more poetic about our native land.

It's been tried many times. The first book on the subject that I remember reading was Bruce Hutchison's *The Unknown Country*,[1] which time has not made less beautiful than it was in 1942. His book spoke of many things, but at heart it was a hymn to rural values: "Can we not hear the sound of Canada? Can we not hear it in the rustle of yellow poplar leaves in October, and in the sudden trout-splash of a silent lake, the whisper of saws in the deep woods, the church bells along the river, the whistle of trains in the narrow passes of the mountains, the gurgle of irrigation ditches in the hot nights, the rustle of ripe grain under the wind and the bite of steel runners in the snow?"[2]

There have been many more efforts to define the country. George Grant's *Lament for a Nation*,[3] published in the '60s, was a requiem for the passing of conservative values. More recently Richard Gwyn's *Nationalism Without Walls* urged us to stand strong against the rising winds of globalization and Americanization.[4] These are just three of many efforts that have been made to pin down the *Canadian* identity in a way that will appeal to our emotions.

The trouble is that these books tell us a lot about Hutchison, Grant, and Gwyn, but they don't tell us much about *Canada* – even less if you try to fit the three of them together. Even as descriptions of a particular moment in our history they always leave somebody out of the picture, and the passage of time takes an additional toll. Today's diesel locomotives do not whistle, nor do our chainsaws whisper, and there are quite a few *Canadians* who don't agree with Mr. Gwyn about the evils of globalization.

The insights of these writers are valuable to us because they are personal. They touch each of us differently and can help us to define ourselves as individuals. But being *Canadian* is another matter. We can't insist that our fellow citizens embrace these memories and visions. If we are seeking the universal and the timeless in the *Canadian* identity we will have to settle for less – and it will have to be expressed in prose.

One way to get at the essence of our identity is to consider what we are not. To start with I believe it would be a very good idea for us to put aside the notions that *Canada* is a corrected version of the U.S.A., or that its identity can be found in our geography.

We're Not Improved Americans

Many of our efforts to define the *Canadian* identity have concerned themselves with how we differ from the Americans. A commonly held idea is that we are a kinder, gentler people than our southern neighbours, because we have, for instance, less crime, and universal health care.

There is even some scholarship on the subject. Perhaps the most extensive book on the differences between *Canadians* and Americans is *Continental Divide*, by the distinguished American political sociologist Seymour Lipset.[5] Lipset concludes that the essential difference is summed up in the goals expressed by the founding fathers of our two countries. The United States is organized around the principle of "life, liberty and the pursuit of happiness" while the Canadian nation was founded to provide us with "peace, order, and good government."

Lipset's central argument, which follows from this distinction, is that "Canada is a more class-aware, elitist, law abiding, statist, collectively-oriented and group-oriented society than the United States."[6] What does this mean in practice? Not very much, I think.

I have always felt that *Canadians* do not differ significantly, perhaps not at all, from Americans. This perception may have a lot to do with where I come from: I spent my childhood in a region very close to the U.S. border. (When you think about it, this is true for most *Canadians*.) In my case, the state on the other side of the "line" was Vermont.

I have an uncle and aunt who lived for many years on a street in Beebe, Quebec. The north side of this street, and all the houses on it, are in Canada. And facing them, on the south side of the street, the houses are in Beebe, Vermont. The street is named – you guessed it – Canusa, and the white line painted down the middle of Canusa Street, to separate the traffic, serves very nicely as our international border. Those who live in the area do notice some differences between Beebe, Canada and Beebe, U.S.A. – the price of chickens and gasoline, for instance. But if you get to know the people in the two Beebes you will find it hard to believe that the folks to the north of the white line are more "class-aware, elitist, law-abiding and collectively oriented" than their neighbours on the other side of the street. They are, for all intents and purposes, indistinguishable. That's the way it is in Beebe.

Some people get upset when I use this story as an indication that Americans and *Canadians* don't really differ all that much. They say, "That's Vermont. Vermont is not like the rest of the United States."

Well, that's the point. Vermonters are special, and so are New Yorkers, and Texans, and the folks in Utah. If you compare an afternoon in Rosedale with an evening in the Bronx you're going to turn up some differences. But I'm convinced that if you took an unsentimental look at life in a dozen towns spread throughout the U.S.A. and *Canada*, talked to the people in the local Wal-Marts, you'd have a hard time telling which ones belong to us and which belong to them.

Lipset's book is a gold mine of information on the way Americans differ from Canadians: Belief in God – Americans 95 percent, Canadians 86 percent; Satisfied with job – Americans 69 percent, Canadians 63 percent. Other observers have noted that American shopping malls are overheated and that they serve larger portions of food in their restaurants. But there doesn't seem to be much you can actually do with this information. And you are left with the feeling that you'd get the same kinds of differences in a survey comparing Newfoundland with British Columbia, or California with Nebraska, or big cities with small towns anywhere. Yes, their ancestors were revolutionaries and ours were counter-revolutionaries. But these ancestors had an awful lot in common as well. Read about what brought them here, and how they lived, and you'll see what I mean. Lipset's work is interesting and so, perhaps, are the five hundred references in his bibliography. But I don't think that his public-opinion polls provide raw material for an answer to the identity question that would satisfy many *Canadians*.

When it comes right down to it, American culture is *Canadian* culture too. The artists who create the Hollywood images that define America for most of us are just folks from small towns and cities in both the U.S.A. and *Canada*. What they do is not American. It's just plain popular. American movies are being filmed every day in the streets of Toronto and Vancouver. And Universal Pictures is controlled out of a small office on Peel Street in downtown Montreal.

The attempt to define ourselves in terms of the United States has a couple of other disadvantages. If we insist we're different because of our health services, what happens if ours get worse and theirs get better? Americans already spend 80 percent more per person on health care than we do, and their system, like ours, is changing rapidly.[7] It appears that the United States currently has more murders but rape is more frequent in Canada. What happens if next year the figures are reversed? Do we lose our identity? Isn't it a good idea to be "kind and gentle" in terms of some more enduring criteria than the figures of the United States Bureau of Statistics?

Seeing ourselves as a better kind of American also has the disadvantage of providing *Canadian* demagogues with a fertile breeding ground for all kinds of anti-Americanism, carefully crafted to advance the cause of some interest group or off-load the responsibility for a local catastrophe. And we have risen to the challenge. In a recent book, *Yankee Go Home*, the historian J. L. Granatstein has traced the history of this phenomenon and it is not a pretty thing to see.[8] John Diefenbaker emerges as the modern champion of anti-Americanism but he has plenty of company.

So a definition of *Canadians* should, in my opinion, make no reference to the United States. I presume – I hope – that the people of Uruguay don't need to know why they are not Argentinians. Let's find out who we are rather than who we're not. We should compare *Canada* with standards we set for ourselves.

GEOGRAPHY

The Canadian Prime Minister never tires of reminding us that the Rocky Mountains are a part of our national identity. On the other hand, a former Quebec premier, Jacques Parizeau, says his first glimpse of these same Rockies persuaded him that Quebec didn't even belong in this country. The rest of us will be pardoned for seeing all this as political hyperbole. *Canada* is not defined by its geography. In fact, our geography is one of the things that divides us.

It's nice to have Mount Assiniboine and Peggy's Cove within our borders but if someone prefers Mont Blanc and Old Orchard they're no less *Canadian* for that. Most of us will never see the whole country – many will pass our lives within the confines of a small community. If I were to base my own nationality on geography I would need an Eastern Townships passport, because this region, its villages, streams, and hills, is about all I possess by way of emotional attachment to a locality.

Some other *Canadians* – both poets and comedians – have suggested that it's our climate which defines us, that we are all somehow united around the idea of snow. This notion probably springs from some people's memories of childhood on the prairies. But there are unlikely to be many subscribers to that vision among the Sikhs in the underground shopping corridors of downtown Toronto.

It's possible that all Tunisians have the desert as part of their collective identity. Perhaps the Swiss are a mountain people. But *Canada* has too much geography; there's no one feature we have in common. Efforts to unite us around the land inevitably end up in appeals to "unity in diversity" and I'm afraid that's not good enough.

When you think about it, our two longest stretches of border aren't defined by geography either. Half of our southern frontier is an artificial construction on the forty-ninth parallel of latitude, and as far as I know there isn't even agreement on the location of our northern border. *Canada* cannot be found by looking at a book of photographs. In the words of Rick Salutin, "Sometimes a trip across the country is just a trip across the country."

Canada: No Founding Anything

Canada is not an improved version of the U.S.A. – and we won't find out who we are by looking at the scenery. Furthermore, I'd like to suggest that *Canada*, neither nation-state nor society, is not united around its founding nations, its two official languages, or a common culture.

THE FOUNDING NATIONS

In an earlier chapter about Quebec we recalled the origins of the idea that *Canada* is the constitutional property of two founding nations: the French-speaking and Catholic descendants of European settlers from France, and the English and Scottish – and Protestant – descendants of settlers from Britain. Some people seem to believe that our country should be based on the values of these two groups, and that the government has a mandate to make sure that everyone else integrates into one or the other of these societies.

This argument may be useful for francophone Quebecers in their attempt to justify special-member status in the federation. But for the other founding nation it has no meaning. No one in the other nine provinces is interested in building a society based on the Protestant values of true-born Englishmen. *Canada* is a country of minorities. The British, for the moment, form the biggest single group. But the day is long past when they could claim a privileged position. The Constitution still proclaims our purpose to "promote the interests of the British Empire" and the British monarch is still our head of state, but these things will shortly pass because no one takes them seriously. They have no influence at all on the development of public policy in *Canada*.

Canada's two largest urban centres, Toronto and Vancouver, have the highest proportion of foreign-born residents of any cities in North America, and we are all evolving into ways of life that make little or no reference to the unique culture of the British Isles. There is no longer any interest on the part of the United Kingdom to create a society here in its own image. Britain's equivalent of Charles de Gaulle does not exist. To be precise, about 22 percent of *Canada* is of British origin, and 3 percent is French.[1] That leaves 75 percent of the population with other ethnic ties – Asian, Latin American, African, European. Perhaps it's time to give them a break. There is no reason for *Canadians* to go along with the idea that there are two ethnic groups whose birthright gives them a special position within our country.

For *Canada*, the Two Founding Nations theory is irrelevant. It flies straight in the face of reality – and it crashes. Even if you cling to the idea that, once upon a time, there really were two founding nations, you are forced to admit that only one of them is left – and it's living in Quebec.

LANGUAGE

It makes no more sense to talk of two founding languages, or of its offspring, official bilingualism.

The contemporary concept of a bilingual *Canada* was a creation of Pierre Trudeau. In response to growing nationalism in Quebec in the '60s, he came up with the proposition that people should be able to live in English or French in any part of the country. And he proposed to achieve this through public policy. As myth it has captured the imagination of thousands of *Canadians* of good will. As a political goal it was dead on arrival.

The problem stemmed from the premise that there could be some kind of symmetry between the two languages. This might make sense if we were talking about languages of reasonably equal importance, say French and German in Switzerland. But to state that English and French are both languages of America is roughly equivalent to saying that the London taxi and the Airbus are both means of transportation. It's true but it's irrelevant. These two languages have their modern origins in Western Europe, they are both relatively easy to learn, and each has inspired a rich literature – and that's about all they have in common.

French is a regional language that is declining in importance. It is essential for life in France and parts of Belgium, Switzerland, and Quebec. It's also useful in some former French colonies, although even there it is slowly being replaced by English. In the rest of the world it is of literary interest only. If Spanish were the first language of Quebec an interesting dynamic might have been created in the Americas, but you can travel from the Arctic to Tierra del Fuego without having to speak a word of French – except in Quebec.

English, on the other hand, is a word for two different things – a regional language and a global means of communication.

And in both respects it's increasing in importance. As a language it is necessary in the United Kingdom and in many of its former colonies, notably the United States. In the U.S. and Canada combined it is the first language of 98 percent of the population – there are only 6.5 million people who can't speak any English in this vast area, and 4 million of them are in Quebec.[2] As a means of communication, English is used globally by millions of people who have no interest at all in Shakespeare but want to sell tractors, negotiate a treaty, or talk to room service in a Japanese hotel. It has become the easiest language in the world to speak badly. This does not make English-speaking people superior in any way to other people, but their language is superior to French in the same way that a word processor is superior to a typewriter.

The people of Quebec want to retain French as their principal language. If we assume their education policy to be a reflection of the popular will, it appears they want French to be the only language spoken. They hold that speaking French is "a manner of conceiving one's existence."[3] As a result of this policy 70 percent of Quebec's francophone population speaks no English today;[4] in Montreal alone there are 1.3 million people who speak only French. In the light of continental realities this may seem foolish, not a policy to be visited on your children, although it's still a legitimate goal of public policy if that's what everybody in Quebec wants.

But in terms of a Canada-wide policy it should be evident, even to the casual observer, that a plan to make French and English official languages and treat them as if they were the same thing – coast to coast – flies in the face of reality. Pierre Trudeau's decision to make Ottawa bilingual was understandable. But his project led people to believe it should be possible to live in French in British Columbia and had the effect of creating far more tensions than it resolved.

Official bilingualism has inspired unfair comparisons by both English and French Canadians. English Canadians complain that Quebec is the only place where one of the two official languages is suppressed. And francophones argue that the English in Quebec are Canada's best-treated minority. Everybody's right. But the difference in the two languages makes the comparisons pointless.

English is the common language of our country. But *Canada* is not defined by it any more than Colombia is defined by Spanish. English happens to be our official language here for two very good reasons: 85 percent of the population are using it every day;[5] and we certainly could not find a better way to communicate with the rest of the world.

French need not be an official language. To be blunt about it, French today is a marginal, strictly local language in *Canada*. Even after thirty years of artificial respiration, only 588,585 *Canadians* are currently using French as their main language. With no encouragement at all, 553,045 other *Canadians* are using Chinese.[6]

Canada is not the home of the two founding languages, or even one of them, and the country has no need for a language debate. Some might feel this alone justifies Divestiture.

CULTURE

There are some people who believe that *Canadians* are, or should be, united by a common culture that our governments have an obligation to illustrate and develop. What, exactly, do they mean? Unfortunately, most of us don't have the faintest idea.

Along with "nation" and "people," "culture" is the most abused word in the lexicon of Canadian politics. Those who seek refuge from this confusion in the dictionary will discover that it is simply "a particular form or type of intellectual development."[7]

Presumably this would be a product of all the forces that touch on our intellect and our imagination – religion, language, family, community customs and traditions, the arts, popular entertainment, and a host of other influences including the cultures of our neighbours and our ancestors. Most of us would believe – or hope at least – that our country's politicians and bureaucrats play a minor role in our personal cultural development.

This is not the case in Quebec. Its cultural policy is based on the notion that speaking the French language is "not just a means of expression, but a medium of living as well . . . an institution, a way of life."[8] Its intellectual elite is obsessed with finding out "who we are" and encouraging everyone to share the vision. They believe that the state should take the lead in this adventure.

Efforts to define this distinctiveness always get bogged down in the details. For instance, it is argued that French Quebec is typified by a Latin *joie de vivre* – but French Quebecers are no more Latin than their Norman ancestors. Some argue that the French culture of Quebec is illustrated by its unique *Code Civil*. But this code produces outcomes that are indistinguishable from those of the common law. The celebrated *Caisse de dépôt et placement* turns out to be nothing more than a way of managing public pension funds that is used in many other countries. The co-operative movement, popular in Quebec, is just as popular in Saskatchewan. Quebec's traditional culture was strongly influenced by the Roman Catholic Church but these traditions are seldom respected today. Montreal has a symphony orchestra, a ballet, museums, and an opera. The very existence of these institutions is seen as an expression of Quebec's cultural distinctiveness. But similar institutions are to be found in every town of equivalent size in North America.

The annual outbreak of schizophrenia over the choice of floats in Quebec's National Day parade is the most poignant illustration of contemporary Quebec's difficulty in defining its distinct culture.[9] Undaunted, the effort continues and every new immigrant is requested to embrace the French language, not only for purposes of communication, but as "the common civic value."[10]

In *Canada*, cultural policy has much more limited objectives. In fact it attempts to address only two aspects of our culture: the arts and popular entertainment. Public funds are provided for the promotion of theatre, radio and television programs, music, dance, painting, and regional festivals, and controls have been established which attempt to limit the influence of the popular entertainment industry – films, magazines, television – of our neighbours to the south. This is the extent of our explicit cultural policy.

Is there more than this to *Canadian* culture, and should the government play a role in defining it? Proceduralists would answer No. They would argue that, in a state devoted to individual liberty, we should assume that people are able to make their own choices when it comes to religion, language, traditional and family ties, self-development, and all the other allegiances that go into each person's intellectual development. Culture is personal, specific to each person. The government should have nothing to say about whether we are supposed to prefer Philip Glass to the Spice Girls, or the study of history to a course in computer programming.

However, it's not this simple in practice. Our political structures are a reflection of a cultural orientation. And our governments, federal and provincial, are properly involved in all kinds of activities that go beyond the sponsorship of the arts, and that require decisions that may have an impact on our intellectual development. The educational system is an obvious example. So governments cannot avoid a cultural bias, be it explicit or implicit.

But *Canada* as a whole can entertain no hopes for an all-encompassing cultural identity. It's a useless enterprise for our politicians and bureaucrats to go in search of it, and the country would be the poorer if they were to succeed. *Canada*'s founding nation, the British, does not insist that its way of life be defined as the official culture of the country. There is a widespread belief that people of all origins should play a role in the evolution of our identity and that the English language is not a tool for collective cultural development, but rather a playing field on which more interesting aspects of each individual's personality can flourish.

Furthermore, our far-flung political boundaries make the undesirable impossible. We are not a people or a single society and there's no point in trying to correct this situation. Every effort to reinforce Anglo-Saxon virtues, or impose a new definition of who we are, based on Asian values or the American way of life, is doomed to failure. Our culture as individuals, our intellectual development, will evolve in unpredictable ways and our government will simply try to reflect this evolution. This is the way *Canadians* want things to be and they understand instinctively that no other way is possible. So, for *Canadians*, cultural policy, wherever it appears, will be a reflection of what we are today, neither an extension of what we were nor a vision of what we might become. And its application will be limited to specific areas of public policy that must be public for other reasons.

Ray Conlogue in his book *Impossible Nation* points out that Canada's English-speaking majority has "failed to develop a cultural identity commensurate with the possession of a nation state."[11] To which we can only add, "Thank God." There is no founding culture to be defended in *Canada*. There is no founding anything.

The *Canadian* Identity:
A Moral Bond

If geography, language, culture, ethnic origin, and religion can't tell me anything about my country, what's left? There's a lot left, and I think you will like what you find here. But before we take a closer look, let's recall the limits of the enterprise.

A definition of *Canada* must be one that is understood and accepted by all of us, descendants of Europeans who have been here for many generations, and immigrants from other countries who became citizens only last week. It can't apply only to people who have travelled coast to coast: it has to mean something to those who have never left their village. It can't be just for fans of CBC Radio 2; it has to be felt by kids on motorbikes. So, if *Canada* is to be defined in a way that will be understood and accepted by everyone who lives here, it must be defined narrowly.

I understand and sympathize with those in the salons and the political corridors of our country who search for meaning and national identity by examining their personal lives and observing the activities of those around them. I've spent many hours engaged in this activity myself. There is no harm in debating whether hockey is our national sport, or compassion our national virtue. This is conversation. The problem only arises when we insist that the government adopt these objects of our affection, make them official. I'm talking about everything from a national flower to a national religion. Before we adopt one of these, I think we have a responsibility to make sure it fits us all. If we respect this rule when choosing our national symbols, we aren't going to have many of them.

I recently found myself seated at dinner with a family from Estonia, elderly mother and middle-aged son with his wife. They spoke to each other in Estonian but to me in English. Canadian citizens, they have been here for over thirty years. The reason they left home is that in the '40s, Estonia was invaded by Russians, Germans, and then by Russians again, in the space of six years. Many of their friends and relatives were killed or removed to Siberia. This family reached Canada by way of Finland, Sweden, and England, living hand to mouth in each of these places. I asked them what Canada meant to them. They did not mention the Canada Council or even the CBC. The answer came spontaneously and in one word – *safety*.

Canada is about politics, politics only. It's a federal constitution, two orders of parliamentary government and, as the Supreme Court has put it, "the global system of rules and principles which govern the exercise of constitutional authority in the whole and in every part of the Canadian state."[1] If you seek to discover everything there is to know about yourself in this you will be disappointed. *Canada* cannot provide you with a complete identity, just a few bits and pieces. There are too many different regions here, too many peoples, too many cultures. *Canada*'s residents are free to decide with their neighbours whether they form a nation, constitute a distinct society, want to speak this or that language. *Canada* says "be our guest – but don't expect the state to take sides or even get involved in these

debates." It will not be involved in the "sentimental preoccupations of its constituent peoples." There's no single definition of
our society which would satisfy all *Canadians* and, in any event,
Canadians are free to change their mind on these subjects at any
time without giving prior notice.

This limited definition of *Canada* leaves a whole lot of
space for the exercise of our freedom as individuals. The shape
of that freedom need not concern us here; there can be 22
million different configurations. Our task is to define the much
more limited sense of collective responsibility that defines the
Canadian community.

Let's start with our Constitution.[2] We have shared the same
basic Constitution for 130 years, which is almost a world record.
The original document, a simple Act of the British Parliament,
is the ultimate proceduralist constitution. No organizing
principles are invoked. Four provinces, Ontario, Quebec, New
Brunswick and Nova Scotia, are joined in a political union. The
purpose: "to conduce to the welfare of the provinces and
promote the interests of the British Empire." That's all it said
about a *raison d'être* then, and that's all it says today. There is no
mention of an underlying political philosophy.

The document provides that *Canada* is to be governed democratically, although exactly who should be allowed to vote is
not specified. And, recognizing the diversity of our regions, a
federal system was established. The central Parliament, with its
two Houses, reflects this preoccupation, as does the attribution
of important responsibilities to the provincial governments.
This division of powers is quite precise, for the times at least.
"Beacons, Buoys, Lighthouses, and Sable Island" are to be a
federal preoccupation; "Shop, Saloon, Tavern and Auctioneer
licences" are to be dispensed by the provinces. The rest of the
document is mostly housekeeping: the languages that can be
used in the courts, guarantees for religious education, the salary

of the Governor General, lumber dues in New Brunswick, the promise to construct a railway to Halifax. A specific provision is made for the possible addition of new provinces.

The original Constitution has had minor modifications over the years. And quite recently, in 1982, some fundamental changes took place. The British Act of Parliament was patriated to Canada, universal suffrage was confirmed, and a section on the official languages was added, along with a formula for amending the Constitution and a commitment to alleviate regional economic disparities. Most importantly, a Canadian Charter of Rights and Freedoms, designed to protect the individual from his or her government, was inserted in our Constitution. Most of these rights existed already, implicit in our common law, but the effect of putting them in writing was to further diminish the credibility of those who believe that the state should legislate a common vision of the good life.

There have been some criticisms. It is argued that the Charter places too much power in the hands of the courts. And, despite its new focus on the individual, the document has inspired an astounding amount of collective activity, by interest groups representing communities which feel that our society discriminates against them. But the people of *Canada* are very favourably inclined toward the Charter. In public opinion surveys it ranks above all other institutions and symbols as the most important national invention – even ahead of the Mounties.[3] It puts in writing something that seems to be consistent with the way we want to live. Faithful to the vision of its creator, Pierre Trudeau, it is a solemn declaration of independence from mere ties of nationality.

What is the moral code on which this enduring *Canadian* civil association has been built? It is a set of standards – important but limited – for political action. It does not provide guidance on how to live, be successful, or happy. It establishes a community, a body of people living in the same locality. It tells us very little about the nature of that community. The *Canadian* moral code does not propose an ideology. It does not make us a caring society, or a selfish one. It doesn't even create a society. It does not define public morality. The Constitution is a system, a framework which enables all kinds of public policy to be developed and implemented, based on the will of the people who live here. It's a playing field with some rules of the game. But it doesn't tell us who is supposed to win. Nothing a *Canadian* does can be un-*Canadian*, unless it's unconstitutional. The *Canadian* Constitution is designed for a society in motion, for people who "prefer the road to the inn."

It's a forum we have created to permit us to continually redefine our private space and our mutual responsibility in terms of concrete issues. Take, for instance, some current questions of public policy. *Canadians* are divided over whether people should have the right to end their own lives or the lives of their unborn children. They don't agree on the precise point at which income-support programs begin to erode the lives of the families they have been designed to help. Does a government subsidy create meaningful work for someone in Lethbridge, or is it just a corporate rip-off? There are no answers to these questions that would satisfy everyone, and none will be found in the Constitution. What that document provides is some rules for dealing with these questions peacefully and democratically, so that the consensus can be understood and accepted by everyone.

On the broader issues of income redistribution, some *Canadians* believe that more government services should be provided, and taxes raised to make them possible. Others think taxes are too high and that wasteful public services should be eliminated. The only way to measure the current trade-off on these issues is by looking at the proportion of our Gross

Domestic Product that is collected in taxes and redistributed by the state. Today the figure is about 45 percent. But if it were to go up to 60 percent, or down to 30 percent, we'd still be *Canadians*.

However, this is not just a procedural society. A moral code is firmly embedded in the *Canadian* constitutional document. The first and most important element of this code is the idea that we are in a state of mutual allegiance with everyone who lives within *Canada*'s borders, not with the objective of achieving a common substantive purpose, but through loyalty to the structures that provide us with our freedom and its corresponding responsibilities, in the words of Michael Oakeshott, to "the authority of certain conditions in acting."[4] Those of us who have been here for a long time tend to take this for granted but it is a priceless asset. It is this structure that inspires millions, among them my Estonian friends, to risk everything they have to be with us. Our loyalty to it finds its expression in a number of symbols – our flag, national anthem, national holiday – and in a sure solidarity with our fellow citizens.

The second element of this code is expressed in the federal nature of our political structures. It's an understanding that, in recognition of our widely dispersed population, local matters should be decided locally. If you move from one part of *Canada* to another you have to expect that things are going to be done differently. But there is also an understanding, reflected in the text of the Constitution, that local matters often have a national dimension and that there will have to be co-operation and perhaps even a certain number of overlapping jurisdictions if everyone's interests are to be secured. For instance, we want to have *Canadian* standards for our basic needs: education, health care, income support. And local economic development is reinforced by a clause in the Constitution that commits our central government to equalization payments and a concern for regional disparities.

Canadians identify positively with both of their governments, and see them as two parts of a whole. A precise and permanent separation of powers is not critical, or even possible.
People just want both parts to be effective and efficient.

A third aspect of our moral code can be found in the principles embedded in our Charter of Rights and Freedoms. We have
left room for them to be interpreted by *Canadian* courts in the
light of the evolving values of our society (and attenuated by
our celebrated "notwithstanding clause"). But they speak clearly
of a desire to live in a community that respects our private
space, the right to due process before the law, freedom from
discrimination, and freedom of expression. They also speak of
the responsibilities that accompany each freedom, the understanding that these rights exist only when all citizens apply
them to their neighbour as well as themselves. We hold our
fellow citizens in thoughtful regard not because they are exceptional or because we agree with them, but because they are
fellow citizens.

Finally, the Constitution specifically recognizes one ethnic
group only, the native people, as deserving of special consideration in the conduct of our civil association. In doing this we also
make it clear that no other group, not the founding nations, not
the people of any particular language or race or religion, is entitled to privileged consideration in the conduct of this civil association. With this one exception, the Constitution encourages
the "drowsy non-perception of distinctions"[5] between ethnic
and cultural groups.

A deeply felt commitment of mutual allegiance with all
Canadians; a commitment to parliamentary rule; the search
for fairness in our respect for basic human rights and freedoms;
respect for local and regional values and priorities; above all, a
respect for the Constitution itself – that's what you get from

being *Canadian*. This is our common culture, our civil association. It may not satisfy my definition of what it is to be *Canadian*. Nor yours. But that's all that *we all* agree on. And it's enough.

Canada is not an *Unknown Country*. It's not awaiting discovery. Its nature is evident and this is frustrating only to those who want to remake the country in their own image. Within its framework we are free – not to build a country, that's not our goal – but to build a life. Together, we have fashioned our political institutions and the moral code which inhabits them. To understand them we don't have to compare ourselves with the Americans or the British or with any other people or place. The institutions have shaped us, we have shaped them, so that over the years they fit.

Are the political structures established in our Constitution perfectly suited to governance in contemporary society? Of course not. The Senate and the House of Commons are imperfect institutions. Their reform is a legitimate subject for public debate. But we understand that we have got to where we are today with these institutions, and that perfection in this matter has not been achieved with any system yet devised. There is no constitutional crisis in *Canada*.

Is the country adequately structured to face the future? Well, the future is unclear. But this is an open and highly educated society with an active and free press, a respected judicial system, freedom of movement for people, goods, and capital, sophisticated monetary and fiscal tools, extensive natural resources, modern means of communication with the rest of the world, a hospitable and respected legal structure, an open economy which is capable of producing wealth, and a relatively civilized policy for redistributing it. There are many problems to be addressed and others we can't foresee will come along. But this country seems as well set up as any to handle its internal problems and adapt to global change, perhaps even to influence it. And there are four vigorous *Canadian* political parties in Ottawa to ensure that all points of view are represented.

This is all we need to know about our country. But we need to know it. And this is the hardest part. If such a country is to work, our leaders must engage themselves actively in formative politics. They must continually define and teach, not patriotism, not memories of our childhood, but something much more important, much better, and much more difficult. They must teach "civic virtues, a politics that cultivates in citizens the qualities of character that self-government requires." They must help us understand the value of a community, with the human being at its centre, united by a process. We have something better than patriotism. We are citizens.

12

The Republic and the Nation

Canada is a "republic," "nomocratic," united around a Constitution and the rule of law. We did not choose each other. Most of the people with whom we share the country are strangers, completely unknown to us. We were told one morning that Newfoundlanders were now *Canadians* and we accepted them. *Canada* represents an effort to secure all its citizens – Sikhs in Toronto, Chinese in Vancouver, Anglo-Saxons in Halifax – an equal voice in their own government. It is the pursuit of fairness for all. It's not a free-enterprise state. It's a "no enterprise" state.

Quebec, on the other hand, is a nation, "teleocratic," a society with final ends to which its residents have been called. In this sense it's not unlike a plantation, or in more contemporary terms, a corporation. Newcomers are expected to "integrate into Quebec society." When defining their society, Quebecers are expected not only to speak the same language, but to say the same thing. It is logical, inevitable, that in such a society any political responsibility that does not reside within the state lies with a "foreign power" and must, eventually, be recuperated.

These two societies do not fit well together. The struggle between Quebec and *Canada* has been going on for two hundred years. In the nineteenth century it became manifest in the efforts to colonize the West, climaxed by the Riel Rebellion. In the first part of this century we witnessed the intense and divisive debates over Canada's participation in the two world wars.

In our contemporary life the hostilities play themselves out in an unending debate over the allocation of powers between the federal and provincial governments. The Canadian Constitution establishes a role for both in the conduct of public policy. But, as in all federal systems, the lines are not clearly drawn. And the vocabulary of our Constitution, while relevant to the values and the technologies of the nineteenth century, doesn't say anything specific about which government is responsible for research and development, or low-income housing, or the Internet. Moreover, the general distinction that guided the framers of the Constitution between local and national matters has become blurred by a greatly accelerated movement of people and information. Canadians can move freely from Calgary to Vancouver. When they do, their expectations about such basic services as health care and pensions and schools for their kids remain unchanged.

The Constitution provides for a federal role in local matters. The central government cannot legislate on local issues but it is free to spend where it wishes and it has broader and more powerful taxing powers than the provinces. The people in every province except Quebec believe that the federal government should play a role in developing national standards in such "local" matters as education, health, and social security. They believe that these issues should be dealt with pragmatically. And the people of Quebec disagree, have always disagreed, and there is no indication that they will ever change their minds. It's a question of principle.

The most recent efforts to usher in a new era of co-operative federalism between the provinces and Ottawa were described in the *Globe and Mail* on May 11, 1998, as follows: "All the provinces except Quebec have agreed in principle that while areas such as health, education and welfare are exclusive provincial jurisdiction, the federal government should play a role in defining national standards. The principle embraces a vision in which provinces and Ottawa work as one to offer a more efficient form of national government. . . . Quebec's Minister of Intergovernmental Affairs condemned Ottawa's intrusion into provincial jurisdiction. . . . He said Quebec could never accept Ottawa having a role in defining Quebec's social policy. . . . And there is no government in Quebec, from Duplessis on to today, that could accept such a role. . . . Quebec has refused to attend the talks, sending only observers."

In the event Quebec did attend the negotiations. But when they were concluded Ottawa had signed the social-union pact with the other nine provinces only. The premier of Quebec said he could never go along with such an idea, and the leader of the Quebec Liberal Party agreed with him.

Let's take another example. In late November, 1997, a Royal Commission under the chairmanship of Mr. Justice Krever presented its findings on how 2,500 Canadians came to be infected with the AIDS and hepatitis viruses from tainted blood supplied by the Red Cross. In response, the Canadian government announced that it would set up a new national agency. At the same time Quebec's Minister of Health announced that his province would not participate in the national agency, and that a "Quebec solution," to be announced later, would be developed.

No one knows whether the new Canadian system for blood collection and distribution will be better than the old one. And it's quite possible to imagine that Quebec, or any other province for that matter, could come up with an excellent solution to the problem. But those issues of effectiveness did not enter into the Quebec Health Minister's evaluation of the situation. His statement was based on a political fact of life in his province. Health care is defined in the Constitution as a matter of provincial jurisdiction. Consequently, there must never be a national initiative in this field of activity. Every effort along these lines that begins in Ottawa is, by definition, an effort to enfeeble the Quebec National Assembly, and must be resisted.

Now the notion that there could be a uniquely French solution to a blood distribution problem may strike the casual observer as surprising. But, without exaggeration, that's what Quebecers believe.

We're not talking just about the separatists. Only a few weeks before the blood incident the Canadian Finance Minister wondered out loud if it might be a good idea to consider a national history curriculum, and the Quebec Liberal Party spokesman told him to find a seat in the Quebec National Assembly, or shut up. Even Quebec Liberals insist that the central government's role should be confined to international affairs, the currency, and unconditional transfers of funds to the provinces, to be disposed of as the recipient sees fit. The only concession they have made to the establishment of national standards, for anything, is to propose the creation of regular interprovincial conferences, which the federal government could attend without the right to vote.[1]

This is not a trivial matter. At stake is the ability of our country to provide the most essential – and costly – public services to the Canadian community in a fair and efficient way. Public opinion in *Canada* is supportive of the idea that the responsibility for this should be shared and worked out pragmatically by our two orders of government. Public opinion in Quebec is unequivocal: Ottawa should not even be involved in this discussion.

And there's the matter of constitutional change. The reforms of 1982, and in particular the adoption of a Charter of Rights and Freedoms, have found widespread acceptance in *Canada*. Quebec has refused to accept them and there's no indication that it ever will. And Quebec's attitude makes further reforms of the Constitution, except those on matters with a strictly local impact, impossible. Any attempt to improve our political institutions will be thwarted, technically or politically, by Quebec's single-minded goal of expanding the space it occupies in our constitutional structures.[2]

These are but examples of a fact of political life in Canada: Quebec sees things differently.

To be sure, every time a premier argues with the federal government it's not grounds for Divestiture. All the provinces are in frequent disagreement with Ottawa, and with their neighbours, and the federal system allows, even encourages, these differences. Sometimes Quebec finds itself in agreement with Ontario or Alberta on a given issue. But its underlying argument is with all of the other nine provinces, all the time, and with the federal government as well. The fundamental difference of opinion is with *Canada*. That's what's behind the pressure for special status.

The other nine provinces are engaged in a permanent debate with Ottawa over the allocation of power, over who's to blame for each local disaster, and who gets credit for the new bridge. But it is a ritual, a ceremony played out within the confines of a system, and with a set of rules that is accepted by all parties. It's like watching lawyers arguing in a courtroom, or people playing hockey. *Canadians* have in mind a role for both of their governments and want things to be worked out on a practical basis. Federalism is supposed to be a two-way street.

For Quebec it's a one-way street. Every gain for the province is a victory, regardless of whether it makes sense. Every gain for the federal government is a humiliating defeat, not just for the government of the day, but once and forever for the Quebec people.

The federal government has been forced into the fray. When considering sensible moves to decentralize – manpower-training programs for instance – they hesitate on the grounds that it would be seen as giving in to the separatists. The whole system of negotiation, which should be a natural one, subject to the normal bargaining process, is distorted by the existence of a nation-state within the federation.

The problem has been exacerbated in recent years by Quebec's attitude toward the English living in Quebec. Canadians from Ontario, the Maritimes, the West move easily from one province to another and still feel at home. But ask them to move to Quebec today and, if they agree to do it, they will tell you that they feel they are about to move to a foreign country. *Canadians* don't understand Quebec and feel no sense of shared values, because this sense of partnership has been systematically diminished by Quebecers themselves. So the idea of a policy of give-and-take between the provincial and central government, so natural to most *Canadians*, simply breaks down when Quebec is added to the equation. The sense of sharing, of fraternity, which is the key ingredient in keeping the country together, does not exist when it comes to relations between Quebecers and *Canadians*.

A nation-state tucked into a civil association. A society obsessed with its language – in a country whose other citizens are as oblivious to the language they speak as to the air they breathe. Each state in a different contract with its people. In theory it shouldn't work.

But that doesn't matter. Modern states have no obligation to political theory. If Canada worked, the practical person could argue that we should leave the theory for consideration at another time.

A very good argument can be made that Canada does work. There's no need to repeat all of the statistics and survey results which demonstrate that we are among the world's most successful countries.

The argument would end there except for one small problem: the people of Quebec don't agree. After a century and a half of efforts to accommodate the French Fact into our constitutional structures and political practices, Quebecers argue that Canada is still unfair – to them. There appear to be only three possible responses: continue to make further accommodations; accept that Quebec will never be satisfied and live with that situation; or ask Quebec to leave.

The key question to be answered here is whether Canada would be an even better place if we were to rebuild it according to Quebec's specifications. But the question cannot even be properly posed because Quebec's specifications are left deliberately unclear. The driving force in Quebec politics is not separatism or a clearly defined association but permanent exploitation of the language and culture issue to increase its own political and economic power. For Quebec there is nothing to be gained from a resolution of the constitutional debate. Recognition of the distinct society would just be the starting point for an endless struggle over what it means in practice.

Perhaps we should just accept that we have to live with the problem forever. The benefits of this approach are evident, and the fact that they are evident is the first argument for the status quo. We are at least dealing with the devil we know. Quebec nationalism creates a whole range of public-policy problems, but at least they are familiar. We have developed a vocabulary and a ritual for dealing with them.

However, I would argue that the underlying political contradictions are so fundamental and so far-reaching that we should not put up with them forever. They poison public discourse in the rest of the country, impede the development of harmonious relations between the increasingly diverse people and regions of

Canada, and I think it is generally accepted that the political uncertainty that underlies the debate has seriously impeded the economic prosperity of all *Canadians*.

If each, or even most, of Canada's other provinces had a comparable ethnic vocation it might have been possible to design a political system – a European-style union perhaps – to unite them in a loose confederation. But, of our other provinces, only New Brunswick has given itself this mission, which it has accomplished quite comfortably by using its existing constitutional powers. No other region or province of Canada has an analogous ethnic mission. In fact, outside Quebec, ethnic missions are seen as downright objectionable.

Can a nation-state exist as part of a larger country devoted to the values of the civil association? Of course it can, and 130 years of Canadian history attest to that possibility. Is it a good idea? No longer, I would argue. For Quebecers it works, but not for *Canada*. It is not enough simply to exist. Maintaining and improving the *Canadian* civil association is a project that is worthy of our commitment. It's a difficult accomplishment – and it's impossible with Quebec.

13

The Process of Divestiture

A rose smells better than a cabbage, but that doesn't mean that it makes a better soup.

The final chapters of this book are meant as a reality check. Once people become convinced that Divestiture is a good idea in theory, they will wonder if it is possible. Some will worry about the issue of physical separation: "Won't the Atlantic provinces become like Bangladesh?" Others will wonder if a smaller *Canada* won't be a poorer *Canada*, or fear that the separation process itself may cause economic dislocation. There are questions about how the process would take place, and about the fate of anglophones and native people in Quebec. And then there is the biggest question of all: how do we convince a majority of *Canadians*, and Quebecers, that Divestiture is in their best interest?

I will address all these practical questions. In a way, they are easier to deal with than the theory of it all because the Quebec separatist movement has already inspired a considerable body of work on how separation could be achieved, and what its costs might be. Much of that information is pertinent even if the situation were to be reversed.

There are no final answers here. The Divestiture movement, once started, will create a new dynamic and inspire unpredictable reactions from its adversaries. However, you will discover that, on closer examination, Divestiture appears to present no more difficulties, create no more uncertainties, than the other options for Canada's future that are on offer today. It is an idea that will have popular support from the outset, and, if a majority of Canadians want it to happen, its accomplishment is quite feasible.

HOW WILL DIVESTITURE AFFECT THE *CANADIAN* ECONOMY?

No one can precisely calculate the economic costs and benefits of Divestiture, just as no one has added up the bill we've all paid for the political uncertainty of the past twenty-five years. This doesn't mean that no one has tried. In fact, a vast literature on the mechanics and the costs of separation is available. Since 1977, both the Yes and No sides in Quebec have commissioned dozens of studies by economists, political scientists, and public servants, seeking to prove that separation will be wildly expensive – or won't cost a penny. Recently a number of more balanced analyses have been prepared by academics from other regions of Canada. And the conclusion one comes to after studying the material is that *Canada*, after Divestiture, should be considerably more prosperous than it is today.

We would be losing a province that is slightly poorer than the country as a whole on a per capita basis. As an economic unit, Canada would lose 25 percent of its population but its GDP would be reduced by only 23 percent. So GDP per person would increase by 3 percent. Federal government revenues and the investment base would be reduced by only 21 percent, and exports by 16 percent. Canada would lose only 15 percent of its territory, even if Quebec separated with its present borders intact. In terms of land mass it would be the world's fifth largest country and would remain one of the wealthiest, with one of the highest standards of living.[1]

Furthermore, there are a number of important economic benefits for *Canada* if Quebec is no longer involved. One of the best sources of information on the subject is a book by the distinguished Quebec economist Marcel Côté, *Le Rêve de la terre promise*,[2] in which Côté calculates the costs of independence for Quebec. He lists and analyses close to twenty problems which will arise with separation, and he attaches a price to them. Some of these, related to monetary policy or rearrangement of the civil service, create roughly equivalent costs for both sides. But there are others he points out that will provide significant benefits to *Canada*.

SAVINGS IN TRANSFER PAYMENTS TO QUEBEC

Since the first referendum in 1980 there have been many calculations of the price paid by Quebecers for federal government services. The results have been critical in shaping public opinion in Quebec on the independence issue. Most Quebecers justify their membership in the federation by the economic benefits it brings. So if they are paying more in taxes to Ottawa than they receive by way of services this is an argument for separation. If the opposite is true, federalists have a useful argument to persuade Quebecers to stay Canadian.

The figure in question is easy to explain but difficult to calculate. What is the appropriate formula for allocating the cost of interest on the national debt between provinces? Which province benefits from the expenses of a Quebec soldier and his airplane based in Alberta? And, of course, the deficit or surplus will vary somewhat from year to year.

Côté has examined all the studies prepared on the subject and has arrived at the conclusion that the rest of Canada has a large annual surplus with Quebec. Each year Quebecers get about $3 billion more in services from Ottawa than they pay for.[3] All but the most partisan analysts now seem to agree that this figure is conservative.[4] Put in headline form, each *Canadian* family of four is currently paying at least $600 per year in federal taxes to subsidize the lifestyle of Quebecers. These families will certainly be able to find other uses for this windfall after Divestiture.

THE ELIMINATION OF SUBSIDIES TO QUEBEC

There are considerable benefits that will accrue from the elimination of certain subsidies to Quebec industry. Côté identifies a number of regulated industries in which the prices charged to the consumer in Quebec are kept artificially low because there is a single rate for the whole country, or for Quebec and Ontario. For instance, he calculates that telephone charges will rise by about 15 percent and natural-gas prices by 10 percent in an independent Quebec.[5] There will presumably be corresponding savings for *Canadians*.

But by far the most important of these potential benefits will come from one agricultural commodity: industrial milk, for which Quebec farmers are now allocated a quota amounting to nearly 50 percent of total Canadian consumption, at artificially elevated prices. It appears that the Quebec farmer will lose about $2 billion per year with the loss of this subsidized market.[6] *Canadian* consumers will save about $1 billion of this if they buy their milk at market prices elsewhere. If *Canada* maintains the subsidies, this benefit will go to the agricultural community in its own country.

ANGLOPHONE MIGRATION

Another substantial benefit that *Canada* can expect from Divestiture is the arrival of tens of thousands of highly qualified immigrants from Quebec.

Basing his analysis on emigration patterns over the past twenty years, and on surveys of intentions, Côté estimates that between 200,000 and 300,000 anglophones and new Canadians – and 50,000 francophones – could leave Quebec in the two to three years following independence.[7] To put the magnitude of this movement in perspective it should be noted that total immigration to *Canada* is currently running at about 125,000 per year. This exodus might be partially offset by Canadian francophones who decide to move to Quebec. But it seems clear that there will be substantial net emigration.

These will be immigrants of exceptional quality. Highly educated at the expense of the Quebec taxpayer, they will be English speaking, already fully integrated into the political and social life of *Canada*, and immediately able to take their place in the economy and create new job opportunities for others. Other countries, notably the United States, will compete with us for these immigrants, but *Canada*, if it adopts the appropriate policies, could attract the majority of them. Their arrival will create an economic boom in the areas where they settle. Many will instinctively think of Ontario as a place to live, but with the appropriate incentives every region of the country could benefit.

NEW HEAD OFFICES

Canada also stands to benefit from increased investment. Most of the head offices of Canadian firms have left Quebec over the past twenty-five years. Divestiture would facilitate the movement of the rest. Côté identifies ten specific cases of large firms that would move, including Air Canada, BCE, Canadian National, Imasco, and Standard Life.[8] In fact, most firms doing business across the country would probably find it necessary to set up their corporate head offices in *Canada*.

The End of Political Uncertainty

The most important economic benefit is one to which no precise figure can be attached. The Divestiture process will create further political uncertainty while it is taking place. And then it will end. The possibility of achieving finality on this issue, the prospect of a country no longer riven by internal division and the threat of separation, will have a positive effect on *Canada*'s economy and its standing in the international financial community. We will still have to compete, remain productive, maintain sensible fiscal and monetary policies. But the handicap of political uncertainty will be gone.

When the first separatist government was elected in Quebec in 1976, the Canadian dollar was worth one dollar U.S. Today the Americans can buy one of our dollars for less than seventy cents. This 30 percent devaluation over twenty years can't all be explained by changes in the price of zinc. Economists will differ on the costs of political uncertainty to Canada over the past two decades. No one will argue that it has been cost-free.

In summary, it is probable that when we get out of bed on the morning after Divestiture we will discover that *Canada* is slightly smaller that it was, somewhat more prosperous, and with slightly lower taxes. Our trading areas will be essentially unchanged and we will be blessed by the arrival of thousands of highly qualified immigrants eager to work with us in taking advantage of the opportunities our country offers. The threat of Quebec separation will no longer be hanging over our heads.

Taken together, these economic consequences of Divestiture represent a substantial benefit for *Canada*. They add nothing whatsoever to the justification of the project, which is based entirely on political incompatibility. We are not doing this for the money. But this analysis will reassure those who fear that *Canada* would be permanently weakened if Quebec were not a member of the federation.

Will the Rest of the Country Break Up?

Some Canadians have expressed the fear that if Quebec decides to separate, the rest of the country could break up. It's all guess-work, of course, and the experts are divided on the subject. However if we, as *Canadians*, decide on Divestiture, there is no possibility of break-up. We would only proceed because we all believe that *Canada* has a new and better project which requires that we get Quebec out of the federation. The decision to stay together precedes the decision to ask Quebec to leave.

However, because the possibility of break-up will be continually invoked by those who oppose our project, it is useful to examine these concerns in a little more detail. They revolve around three notions.

The first is metaphysical. There are still some Canadians who believe that their country is nothing more than a moral covenant between the English and the French, and that Quebec is one of the contracting parties. Therefore it's not surprising that these people equate the secession of Quebec with the break-up of Canada. It's no such thing, of course, and if you seek a once-and-forever confirmation of this you need look no further than the Supreme Court ruling of August 1998 on unilateral secession.[1] The judgement makes it clear that Quebec could leave the federation – *and the federation would still be there*, doing business as before. It even describes how the federation would get Quebec out of its system. Constitutionally speaking, at least, the country certainly does not break up if Quebec leaves.

A second concern is that Quebec's departure would create a hole in the middle of the country. What happens when the Atlantic provinces are physically separated from the rest of Canada?

This problem is one of psychology rather than geography. It's inconceivable that Quebecers would build a wall around their new nation. All over the world, people go through other countries to get to their own. Alaska is an evident example, and every day Americans from Buffalo use Highway 401 to get to Detroit. To be more specific, take a look on a map at the present border between the Atlantic provinces and Quebec. It consists of a 250-kilometre stretch connecting New Brunswick and Gaspé, and the frontier between Labrador and northern Quebec. These are not major connections. Very few of our trips between the two regions cross these land borders. The trains that go every night from Montreal to Saint John, N.B. pass through my hometown of Sherbrooke and then head, peacefully, straight through the middle of the Maine woods.

Furthermore, most of our communication today does not involve surface transportation. On the morning after Divestiture, the view from the kitchen windows in Halifax will be unchanged. Not only will the cars, buses, trucks, and freight trains run as before, Toronto will still be 133 minutes away by air. Ships will continue to sail the St. Lawrence. Phone calls to Winnipeg will still cost twenty cents a minute. The Internet and e-mail will be even faster and easier to use than they are today. Things won't be much different – no need to feel different.

A final note of reassurance: Robert Young has discovered that the physical separation of the Atlantic provinces will not be complete.[2] On Killineck Island, off the northern tip of Labrador, Newfoundland will still be sharing an eight-mile land border – with Nunavut.

A third, and more serious, concern of those who fear the break-up is that Canada may turn out to be a "house of cards," and that the removal of Quebec from the federation will unleash the dogs of separatism in British Columbia and elsewhere, resulting in the complete disintegration of the country. More modulated versions of this scenario would have it that secession will desta-bilize the country by stimulating new incentives to change the balance of powers. It is argued that there will be pressures to create, depending on one's point of view, either a more centralized or more decentralized country. If all this isn't enough to worry about, some think that the huge bulk of Ontario in what will be left of Canada could leave the country seriously unbalanced.

With regard to Ontario it's worth pointing out that while it becomes relatively more important in a Canada without Quebec, so does the rest of the country. And "Central Canada," that perfidious sponge of patronage – and of the resources of the West – gets quite a bit smaller. Here are the figures.[3]

Relative Size By Region
(percent of total Canadian population, 1992)

Region	Now	After Divestiture
Atlantic Provinces	8.5 %	11.3 %
Western Provinces	29.3 %	39.3 %
Ontario	36.5 %	49.3 %
Quebec	25.6 %	0 %
"Central Canada" (Quebec & Ontario)	62.1 %	49.3 %

Divestiture makes every region of *Canada* more important.

As to how *Canada* might reconstitute itself – or fall apart – without Quebec, the various scenarios have been explored by a number of distinguished political scientists.[4] By way of example, Robert Young, in two chapters of his book *The Secession of Quebec and the Future of Canada*, provides us with the complete catalogue of possibilities – from a unitary state through decentralization and a confederal regime, all the way to the creation of nine new American states.[5]

These studies are interesting, but it's all sophisticated guesswork. Alan Cairns in a paper for the C. D. Howe Institute has also reviewed this literature and he concludes that "views on the chances for the ROC's survival, constitutional structure and cohesion share little except their tendency to contradict each other."[6]

In any event, for our purposes it's not necessary to have a view on these matters. If Quebec takes the initiative and decides to secede we are faced with a crisis that is not of our own making. It requires us to react. On the other hand, Divestiture starts from a shared conviction that we have a future together without Quebec. Getting Quebec out of the federation becomes just the first step in the process of renewing our commitment to our civil association. With Divestiture nothing is imposed on us from without. It's a decision we take ourselves and it's preceded by a commitment to stay together based on a shared view of the country and its future. In the process of deciding on Divestiture, Maritimers lose their concerns about the Quebec border, and the size of Ontario is seen simply as material for public debate on constitutional reform.

To argue that *Canada*'s existence depends on the presence of Quebec is to attach a very narrow definition to our country. As a theory, I believe it will not stand careful scrutiny. In practice I know it cannot withstand the determination of *Canadians* that things shall be otherwise.

When we vote for Divestiture we are no longer reacting to Quebec's separatists. We don't need any more speculation on our future because we have taken that future into our own hands. When we begin the negotiations we are prepared. We don't need to know in advance whether *Canada* will become more or less centralized, more conservative or liberal. We are simply reaffirming our commitment to a constitutionally based association, freed at last of the constraints of ethnic nationalism. The debate about how to live within this framework will begin only after Divestiture, and it will be based on the understanding that decisions about the role of the state in our lives emerge from an unending "conversation" between all of *Canada*'s citizens.

In Young's words, *Canada* after Divestiture will be "a viable economic entity."[7] It will also be a very viable country.

15

The Future of the English in Quebec

What will become of the English in Quebec? Can we, in good conscience, throw Quebec's Anglos to the separatist wolves, isolate them, perhaps even strip them of their citizenship? These questions will, justifiably, be on the minds of all *Canadians* of good will as they contemplate the merits of Divestiture. Interest in the question will be particularly intense among the 215,000 English Quebecers who have already left the province, and for many other *Canadians* who have ancestors, relatives, or neighbours who once lived in Quebec.

Of one thing we may be quite sure. English-speaking Quebecers will not instinctively embrace the project. They will have very practical concerns: a possible drop in the value of their homes and businesses, the departure of their friends. When, in 1991, two academics from Calgary speculated that it might be a good idea if Quebec separated, the editor of the Montreal *Gazette* wrote a column suggesting, only half in jest, that they should be shot.[1]

If English Quebecers did support Divestiture they would, in all logic, have to vote "Yes" in the next referendum on separation. We can't expect them to do this. But we do have the right to ask them: "What do you propose as an alternative? And what are your plans, and your children's plans, for your community's future in Quebec?" With very few exceptions, I don't think they have any.

My strong impression is that there is no one left in English Quebec today who believes that their community has a viable future. There are certainly many anglophones who will continue to live in Quebec and enjoy it there. I'm one of them. But it is virtually impossible to find a family whose children have remained, and intend to remain, in Quebec. English-speaking people are not moving to Quebec, unless they are transferred to a specific job, or seeking an education. There has been talk of partition, separating out the English parts of the province into a new political unit if Quebec becomes independent. There's nothing wrong with this in theory. But it's hard to believe that many anglophones would be willing to let politics take up fifty or sixty percent of their daily life for five or ten years, and this is the kind of commitment that would be required to achieve partition. For instance, no one has even begun to consider an appropriate minority-language policy for these new regions. The alternative is too easy: just move fifty miles south, west, or east.

There is no plan to revitalize the anglophone community from within, no desire on the part of Quebec's francophones to see it grow, and no interest by anyone outside of Quebec (the federal government included) to come to the rescue. Every year there is going to be a net emigration from this community.

To fully understand the situation it's useful to take a look at the English Quebecers in more detail, and this is helpful for another reason as well. We will discover that there is, in fact, no English-speaking community in Quebec, and the glorious refusal to form one, in the face of frantic and unceasing efforts by both the anglophone and francophone elite, is an eloquent paradigm of all the justifications for Divestiture.

In our other provinces the millions of *Canadians* who live and work in English have many interests. But one of them is not their "English-language community." They don't get together to discuss what they have in common with other people who happen to be speaking their language. They have better things to do.

The English in Quebec feel the same way. But in 1977 they were told this had to change. The newly elected separatist government had conceived a *"projet de société"* based on the notion of "being French," and to make it jell they needed a corresponding anglophone community, for purposes of contrast, and to provide themselves with an enemy. So some anglophone leaders of good will set out to create this highly artificial community. They failed. Their successors, even to this day, continue to make the effort, and the English of Quebec, just as resolutely, refuse to go along with the idea.

The search for leadership for this project began officially in 1982 with the creation of Alliance Quebec, an association that would officially represent Quebec's anglophones.[2] Over the years its presidents and chairpersons, including Michael Goldbloom, Eric Maldoff, Royal Orr, Robert Keaton, Alex Paterson, William Johnson, and myself, have all offered themselves as leaders of the community. We were not alone. The Quebec Liberal Party tried to be helpful. It elected members from predominately English-speaking ridings who were encouraged to speak for the English: Richard French, Clifford Lincoln, John Ciaccia, Herb Marx, myself in another uniform, and those who have followed. Anglophone protest groups came and went: the most recent,

called the Quebec Political Action Committee, is led by Howard
Galganov. New political parties with an exclusively anglophone
agenda were started. Freedom of Choice, led by Dr. David
DeJong in 1978, was followed by the Equality Party, led at first by
Robert Libman and, currently, by Keith Henderson.

The English in Quebec have had many leaders, but not nearly
enough followers. They have consistently refused to be forced
into a collective for anything other than the preparation of
briefs to the Quebec National Assembly on language laws. And
since these haven't been required for some time it's now impossible to get a quorum for a representative meeting of anglophones in the province of Quebec.

There are, of course, many people speaking English in
Quebec, and they belong to any number of "communities." But
they don't respond well when invited to devote their free time
to participation in the Fellowship of Anglophones. As an aid to
understanding this problem we can identify some of the more
obvious components of the anglophone population in Quebec:

- In Westmount and Montreal's "Square Mile" you will find
  the Anglo-Saxon descendants of the class that is rumoured
  to have ruled Quebec in the nineteenth and the first half of
  the twentieth centuries.
- Throughout Montreal and Laval, especially in N.D.G.,
  Verdun, Lachine, and out into the western part of the
  island, there are thousands of anglophones of more modest
  means, middle-class and blue-collar workers, including
  some who are very poor. Their common tie is that they,
  and often their parents as well, were born in Quebec.
- There is an important Jewish community that speaks
  English. Concentrated in Côte-St-Luc, its members live
  throughout the western part of the island of Montreal.

- Rural anglophone communities exist throughout Quebec and there are still a few towns, such as Aylmer, Lennoxville, and Blanc Sablon, that are predominately English speaking.

The members of these first four groups are the people Quebec's political leaders refer to as "*les anglophones de souche*." However, that's just the beginning of our anglophone directory.

- There is a significant black community speaking English in Montreal, people who came here from the Caribbean Islands, many of whom are third- and fourth-generation Canadians.
- In Montreal and, to a lesser extent, throughout Quebec, there are first-generation immigrants from Europe, Asia, and Latin America, who use a lot of English.
- Most of Quebec's native people use English as a first or second language.
- There are thousands of Quebecers whose mother tongue is French but who use English all or most of the time. There are thousands more who retain French as their home language but use English extensively in their daily lives.
- On the western part of the island of Montreal are several communities where you will find hundreds of English-speaking corporate executives and technicians from other parts of Canada, the U.S.A., and Europe, who have been posted to Montreal for indeterminate periods.
- In downtown Montreal there are thousands of English-speaking students from all over the world, attending colleges and universities.
- There are anglophone academics, artists, and journalists, who have been attracted to Quebec for any number of reasons.

• Tied in with the last three categories there are anglophone wives, and increasingly, husbands, who have come to Quebec to be with their spouses, and some have brought their children.

To complicate matters further it should be noted that most of these anglophones are speaking some French every day, some are speaking French most of the time, others don't speak any French at all, and some are regularly using another language – Inuit, Italian – in their everyday lives. Most of their daily preoccupations have nothing to do with the language issue.

These diverse people are the flesh and blood which make up the people speaking English counted by Statistics Canada in the 1996 census.[3] It's inconceivable that they could be brought together as a community around a common vision of their English language and culture. They wouldn't even answer the phone. And yet in the mind of the Quebec francophone elite they are *les Anglais*, head office in Ottawa, wholly owned subsidiary in Westmount. There's no way the francophone vision of this "collectivity" is going to change, and there's no way the "English" are ever going to conform to it. This is the Quebec dilemma. In microcosm, it's the Canadian dilemma as well.

What's the future of all these English-speaking Quebecers after Divestiture? We can immediately assure them that they will still be *Canadian* citizens and they'll be able to get their passports renewed for the rest of their lives. They can also apply for *Canadian* passports for their children. With these options they will have the best of both worlds. With their *Canadian* passports they will be able to move to any part of the country, any time. Or they can renounce their *Canadian* citizenship and obtain Quebec passports, in which case they can apply to live in *Canada* on essentially the same conditions as Americans. And, in all probability, they will still be welcome to stay and work in Quebec.

What will life be like for the English in an independent Quebec? The first sovereign government will be torn between two choices. There will be pressures to reinforce the French identity of the new country in ways which have not been permitted within the federal Constitution: tightening access to English schools, forbidding the use of English in the legislature. At the same time there will be pressure to encourage anglophones to remain in Quebec because it will be important for the new government to remain credible in the eyes of the international community. Historical evidence suggests that, faced with diametrically opposed views on a delicate subject, the prudent politician will do nothing. The best guess is that the language laws and all the other bits and pieces of ethnic politics that are a feature of Quebec life will remain unchanged, at least during the first years of the regime.

The reaction of English Quebecers to Divestiture will therefore depend greatly on the way they see their present situation. There are, broadly speaking, five quite different attitudes that attract popular support today.

Assimilation. There are some anglophones who are already in the process of assimilating into the francophone community. These include people whose mother tongue is French, a few members of the rural communities, and some newly arrived immigrants, including a number of anglophone professionals. We can assume that, with Divestiture, many of these people will choose to remain in Quebec and some may become Quebec citizens. I estimate that about 10 percent of the anglophone community, roughly 70,000 people, are in the process of assimilation.[4]

Collaboration. People in this group are not going to assimilate. But they have real sympathy for Quebec nationalism and believe that the language laws, apart perhaps from a few details, are reasonable. They like life in Quebec the way it is and have confidence it wouldn't change much if Quebec achieved independence. The group includes some academics, journalists, and prominent members of the Westmount community, as well as the anglophone members of the Quebec Liberal Party. Their critics call them the "lamb lobby." In the event of Divestiture most will retain their *Canadian* citizenship. But they will have confidence in the generosity of the francophone majority of their new country and so it can be assumed that they will stay in Quebec, although their children probably will not. There are about 35,000 anglophones, 5 percent of the total, in this category.

Confrontation. These people object strenuously to the language laws and to Quebec nationalism and believe that somebody, perhaps the federal government, should "do something about it." The "lamb lobby" calls them "extremists." They have created the protest groups and "anglophone rights" political parties of the past two decades and in 1998 they succeeded in wresting control of the English lobby group, Alliance Quebec, from those who believed in collaboration. Many of their members come from the Jewish community and from among the middle-class anglophones of N.D.G. and the West Island. The support for partition is strongest among this group. They will be converted to the idea of Divestiture with great difficulty but most would not choose to live in an independent Quebec. They represent another 5 percent, or 35,000 people.

Exodus. Large numbers of anglophones are already making plans to leave the province. A great many of them are under forty. Some will be going as soon as their study or job in Quebec comes to an end. Others are in various stages of preparation. The members of this group could be in sympathy with the Divestiture project. They certainly will not remain in an independent Quebec. They number about 140,000, or 20 percent of all anglophones.

Concern. Most English Quebecers don't identify with either Quebec nationalism or the anglophone reaction to it. They are too busy living their lives to be involved in the daily details of the debate. They can be found in every one of the anglophone communities, particularly in the business world. They worry about the possible break-up of the country and how it might affect their life and the lives of their families. They neither see nor offer any solution to the problem. The "concerned" have no plans to leave at present but they would probably do so, over time, after Divestiture. They are the largest group, making up about 40 percent (280,000 members) of the English community. Most of Quebec's "allophones," persons whose first language is neither French nor English, would also identify themselves in this way.

The Divestiture project is, admittedly, a heart-wrenching proposition for English Quebecers. It will be vigorously opposed by those who are strongly committed to collaboration, because they believe that the unity debate is good for us all and because they like living in Quebec the way it is now. It will be opposed just as strenuously by those who are strongly committed to confrontation, because they believe that the federal government should put a stop to Quebec's nationalist policies. These two groups number perhaps 70,000, about 10 percent of the anglophone community.

The rest of Quebec's non-francophone population will listen with interest to the arguments for Divestiture and they will become even more thoughtful as they consider the very limited alternatives which are available to them in Quebec if they wish to live in their own language. Some will decide to assimilate into the life of the French-speaking majority there. A significant number, I believe, will be stimulated by the opportunity – for themselves or their children – of participating in the life of a revitalized *Canadian* federation.

16

How Do We Negotiate Divestiture?

The process of negotiating the terms of Divestiture is not entirely predictable. During the debate we can expect to hear from everyone: newspaper columnists, TV talk-show hosts, constitutional experts, think tanks, interest groups, community leaders, stand-up comedians, and politicians – and their views will certainly influence public opinion. Jeffrey Simpson will have a word to say on this matter, as will Brian Tobin and Phil Fontaine. However, thanks to the close vote in the 1995 referendum, Canada's political scientists have been preparing the way over the past four years with some serious analyses, both of the path to follow in the secession process, and of the issues which will subsequently arise. For the purposes of this chapter I am going to rely mainly on three sources:

- *The Secession of Quebec and the Future of Canada* by Robert A. Young.[1] Young is professor of Political Science at the University of Western Ontario. His book takes into account most of the studies on the subject which have preceded it.

- *The Secession Papers,* published by the C. D. Howe Institute, Toronto.[2]
- *Sommaire des études sur la restructuration administrative,* published by the government of Quebec.[3] An extensive study of the consequences of separation for Quebec's public sector.

The decision by Canadians to proceed with the project will simplify the scenarios described in these documents, all of which assume a reluctant Canada faced with an ultimatum from Quebec backed up by a substantial "Yes" vote in that province. Our hypothesis, on the other hand, has Canada taking the initiative, and Quebec persuaded to go along with the idea. Both sides will be committed to the outcome.

No Political Association

The non-negotiable starting point in negotiations for Divestiture must be that there will be no political association of any kind between the two countries. The beliefs which have led us to seek Divestiture are grounded in a conviction that the political values of Quebec are incompatible with those of *Canada.* That is the sole reason for the project. We want this to be clear.

This means that the objectives of some Quebecers, to create a confederation in which the two nations would share some newly designed political institutions – "*d'égal à égal*" – will be a non-starter. There will be no association. Apart from the principle involved, there is no practical reason for *Canada* to share political power with Quebec on any basis other than as one of ten provinces, an idea which has been clearly and repeatedly rejected by all members of the francophone leadership in that province. The structure of the new relationship between Quebec and *Canada* will be essentially the same as the one it has with the United States or Mexico. The political scientist Richard Simeon, in his text for *The Secession Papers*, analyses four possible types of connection between an independent Quebec and *Canada* – including a confederal system – and he concludes that "the most likely relationship between an independent Quebec and the ROC would embody linkages between two states, albeit ones that share a continent and a wide range of common interests."[4] That's exactly what we want. Nothing more.

So far as our trading arrangements are concerned there will be important, but not critical, changes in the present situation. Quebec will no longer be part of the Canadian economic union. But it will become part of NAFTA and a member of GATT and we will support them in these initiatives. Trade with Quebec will become neither more nor less complicated than our trade with the U.S.A.

With these two principles established there are a number of important matters to be negotiated. As they are all revealed and developed in the 367 pages of Young's book it is necessary only to briefly recall them here.[5] Young points out that a relatively small number of issues are at stake – he identifies sixteen – and he believes that they would be resolved rather swiftly – "in the course of a few weeks" – although working out the details would clearly require more time. However, it is reasonable to believe that the whole process of Divestiture could be accomplished in a year to eighteen months.

A negotiating team for the federal side will be created, made up entirely of members of Parliament and the civil service who do not come from Quebec.

1. *The Armed Forces*
The first priority will be to ensure order. The members of the armed forces must be allowed to choose their country of allegiance and reminded of their responsibility to serve the Crown

or Quebec's head of state, as the case may be. The physical assets of the military must be divided.

2. Borders

Young argues that Quebec must become sovereign with its existing borders intact. "No other outcome is feasible if the secession is to be rapid and peaceful." It is up to the Quebec government to make peace with the various partition movements that may arise on its territory. If it fails, and some of these groups make application for admission to *Canada*, their arguments must be heard. But *Canada* will not encourage them. *Canadians* can live with this outcome so far as it concerns the partitionist movements which have sprung up since 1995 in the Montreal and Outaouais areas. However, the issue of the native peoples is more complicated.

3. The Native Peoples

The status, rights, and responsibilities of Canada's native people are the subject of a debate which has been going on for a long time in our country. It will continue, with or without Divestiture. The secession question is going to be just another element in an existing universe of issues. These include the status and continuity of existing treaties, the negotiation of land claims, recognition of the right to self-government and the flow of money and programs to native people.

An examination of the alternatives leads to the conclusion that *Canada* will have to transfer its authority over the aboriginal people living in Quebec and that this new country will clearly have to offer them strong guarantees. To this transfer will be added a number of agreements between the two countries ensuring mobility and granting the right of *Canadian* citizenship to all native people who request it. The negotiations will take place in an environment of strong pressure from the native groups and the international community, and the larger debate over native rights will continue indefinitely, in both countries.

4. Access
Canada will obtain unequivocal freedom of movement between the Atlantic provinces and the rest of *Canada*, by land, sea, and air, for goods and people, including the military.

5. The Debt
The formula for sharing the Canadian debt has been discussed at length in Quebec, most particularly during the referendum debates of 1980 and 1995. The proposals for Quebec's share range from a low of 18.5 percent to a high of 32 percent. Eventually both parties will agree on a figure equal to Quebec's share of the Canadian population, which is about 25 percent.

Young points out that the more difficult issue is to determine how the payments will be made, because at present all this debt consists of obligations of the Canadian government, which have varying maturity dates and important annual-interest requirements. He proposes a number of possibilities to resolve this problem.

6. Assets
The federal government possesses billions of dollars in physical assets of all kinds spread across the country, as well as liquid assets in gold and foreign currencies.

The liquid assets will be allocated on a per capita basis, as will defence materials – ships, tanks, and airplanes – which are movable and, in some cases, located outside the country. Ownership of the other physical assets will be based on where they are located. *Canada* will get the Parliament Buildings. Quebec will acquire the Plains of Abraham.

The Seaway Authority will be reconstituted, free access by the three partners will be reconfirmed, and *Canada* will acquire, by treaty, access to the ports of Montreal and Quebec City, because this will be of benefit to both parties.

7. Environmental Issues

Joint agreements will be worked out, some of them in the framework of existing treaties within NAFTA and the International Joint Commission.

8. Citizenship

Quebecers will have an interim period, perhaps two years, in which to choose their citizenship. In order to retain *Canadian* citizenship they will have to renounce their right to Quebec citizenship. Dual citizenship is presently permitted in Canada in certain cases, but the very large numbers of people who will be involved in the event of Divestiture and the rights that citizens possess, including the right to vote, will make dual citizenship impracticable in this case. Children of Canadians, born in Quebec after independence, will have the right to claim *Canadian* citizenship.

9. Mobility and Immigration

During the two-year interim period, all Quebecers will be free to work in Canada. After that, those who had become *Canadian* citizens can move to *Canada* at any time and seek work anywhere in the country. Holders of Quebec passports will require employment authorization, as Americans do today. Tourists and other visitors from Quebec will receive the same treatment as visitors from the U.S.A. No visas will be required and, if the immigration policies of Quebec and *Canada* remain compatible, it will not be necessary to establish border controls. This compatibility might be achieved by the use of a mechanism similar to the current Quebec-Canada agreement on immigration that has been in effect for fifteen years.

It can be expected that Quebec, for its part, will speedily process any requests from *Canadians* who wish to become Quebec citizens, and will make it as easy as possible for *Canadians* to work and play in the new Quebec.

10. Minority Rights

Each country will have the sovereign right – and responsibility – to determine its policies towards minorities. The most important issues will be the status of the English minority in Quebec, and the francophones in *Canada*. There will be no negotiation on these issues. Quebec and *Canada* will establish their own policies based on their concept of justice, the practicalities, and the reaction of the international community.

11. Quebec's Succession to Treaties

Canada will support Quebec's membership in NATO, the United Nations, NAFTA, GATT, the Auto Pact, defence-sharing agreements with the U.S., and other international organizations and treaties. Where financing of these organizations is involved, the sharing of Canada's current contribution will be negotiated.

12. Commercial and Economic Relations

Canada currently exports 5 percent of its GDP to Quebec and Quebec exports 15 percent of its GDP to *Canada*. So it's in everybody's interest to keep the trade routes open and it is relatively easy to accomplish this. On achieving independence Quebec will adopt *Canada*'s existing trade structure and the two countries will agree not to impose tariffs on each other's products. Quebec will become a member of NAFTA and become subject to all of its rules and mechanisms. Quebec's laws, regulations, and tax structures relating to trade will be harmonized with those of *Canada*. A phase-out period of perhaps three years will be established for the agricultural-supply management systems of the milk, eggs, and poultry sectors.

This will be the starting point from which each country, over time, will adjust its tariffs and trade policies in its own interests, as Canada does today with other countries.

13. Social Entitlements

The two countries will agree on "national treatment" in determining eligibility for social benefits. A *Canadian* citizen living in Quebec will pay Quebec taxes and receive the benefits available under Quebec law. This rule will apply, among other things, to health care, welfare, unemployment insurance, and pensions. An agreement will be necessary on the pension liabilities of federal employees who retire or choose to work in Quebec.

14. The Federal Civil Service

After Divestiture, *Canada* will require fewer civil servants and Quebec will need more of them. From a Quebec perspective the best work done to establish its requirements for additional personnel was completed in 1995 and made public by the government in a document entitled *Sommaire des études sur la restructuration administrative*. The analysis was done for each government activity with a great deal of precision. The conclusion is reassuring.

A sovereign Quebec will undertake to employ all of the federal civil servants now living in Quebec (including the Outaouais), who number 69,670, or about 20 percent of the Canadian total. However, only 57,280 of these people will be required. Quebec will assume responsibility for the balance, who will be phased out over a three-year period as contracts expire, and through resignations and retirements.

We also learn from this document that, as Ottawa's activities are merged with those of Quebec City, the Quebec taxpayer will save $1.619 billion per year from the elimination of duplicated services, and a further $1.309 billion because these services will be delivered more efficiently by Quebecers than by their brethren in Ottawa. This can be pointed out to Quebecers as another reason for agreeing to Divestiture.

Of course, not all civil servants living in Quebec will wish to work for that government, and vice versa. It can be expected that discussions on the transfers will be complicated as the civil service negotiates its own future. However, with Quebec having agreed, a priori, to accept its fair share of the Canadian public service, and in the face of its evident need for experienced personnel, we can expect that this debate will not hold up the Divestiture process.

15. Constitutional Changes

In order to remove Quebec from Canada it's necessary to remove it from the Constitution. The appropriate way to do this is by changing the document using the established amending formulas. The starting point for this process will be agreement by *Canadians* to stick to the point, and leave discussions on other ways in which our Constitution might be improved for discussion after Quebec is gone.

If we agree on these two principles the excision of Quebec is surprisingly straightforward. The process is described by Young and in even more detail by Peter Russell and Bruce Ryder in *Ratifying a Postreferendum Agreement on Quebec Sovereignty* in the C. D. Howe series on secession. Our Constitution embodies five amending formulas. Some changes require the assent of all ten provinces, others can be accomplished with the approval of only five. For a few the assent of a single province is sufficient. But if everyone is in agreement on the objective the job can be completed in a few months.

16. *The Currency and Monetary Policy*
In Young's words, "This is an absolutely crucial issue. The stakes are very high." Others have recognized this and there is now an extensive literature on the subject, including a text by David Laidler and William Robson in the C. D. Howe series, as well as a thorough analysis by Côté in his book and in a subsequent monograph.[6]

The goal of everyone is to make sure that the insecurity inside Quebec resulting from its new political status does not give rise to a currency crisis in Quebec, and in *Canada* as well. And whether or not this crisis occurs is dependent on decisions over which neither government has any real control. They can forbid the movement of cars and chickens across their borders, but not the movement of money and other financial assets.

After an analysis of several options, Young comes to the conclusion that the most likely scenario is a common currency, the *Canadian* dollar, with a single central bank under joint management. Laidler and Robson appear to agree but point out that it will impose some very uncomfortable disciplines on Quebec. Côté believes that Quebec will eventually have to establish its own currency, at considerable cost.

The subject is extremely complicated but the issues are becoming clearer day by day as the debate develops. It is evident that *Canada*'s currency could be affected, along with Quebec's, during the Divestiture process, and it is in the interest of both parties to work together and ensure a transition period that inspires the confidence of the world's financial markets.

The example of the Euro is before us. On January 1, 1999, some of the most important currencies in the world disappeared, to be replaced by a new money, controlled by a new central bank. The change was made with the collaboration of the countries involved, in a public and transparent process, in full consultation with the world financial community. The result was satisfactory. There is a lesson here for *Canada* and Quebec.

After an interim period, the value of each country's currency will depend on its own political stability, the quality of its fiscal and monetary management, and the strength of its economy. We can be hopeful that *Canada*, on all these counts, will emerge stronger than it is today.

These are the sixteen issues which must be settled during the process of Divestiture. There are only sixteen. They are known in advance and we are already beginning to figure out how to resolve them. The consensus is that they pose no serious impediments to Divestiture, certainly not if both sides have the same ultimate objective. The basic work in each case could be completed over a few months.

Of course, there will be economic costs associated with the process of Divestiture, tensions will be created, the public sector will put in some overtime. But these costs and tensions will be more acceptable than the ones we endure today in Canada's unending unity debate, because we have the assurance that, this time, they will come to an end.

How Do We Persuade *Canadians* That This Is a Good Idea?

In 1960, Marcel Chaput and a few friends in Montreal started the "Rassemblement pour l'indépendance nationale" (RIN), and on that date separatism in Quebec was transformed from an idea into an institution. At the time, supporters of the movement could fit themselves comfortably into a church basement. Six years later, as a political party, the RIN got 6 percent of the popular vote in a general election. Ten years after that, in 1976, a separatist party was elected to power in Quebec. However, almost forty years after the independence project was conceived, it remains unrealized.

Opponents of separatism would argue that it was a bad idea to begin with, and will never work. Supporters would certainly point to the substantial progress that has been made to date. For those who are attracted to another project – Divestiture – the message is clear. Efforts to gain acceptance must be undertaken with humility and patience.

This chapter should be understood as the first word, not the last, on how Divestiture might take hold of people's imagination and be seen as a serious alternative in our search for solutions to Canada's existential dilemma. We can hope that the idea will, over time, attract a level of energy and commitment to match that of the supporters – theoreticians and practitioners – of separatism.

As it is unlikely that any important political party in Canada, national or provincial, will be prepared to adopt Divestiture as part of its official policy in the months ahead, a movement must be formed as quickly as possible. It's difficult to predict how this will emerge but its founders will discover that there is already a promising nucleus of support for the idea. For over fifteen years, Environics Research Group, one of the country's most respected public-opinion firms, has been asking Canadians outside Quebec about their preferred constitutional options. The most recent of these polls, taken in July 1998,[1] asked the following question: "Here are some constitutional options which have been proposed for Quebec. Which one do you think would be best?" The list of options and the answers are as follows:

Present status in Canada	77 %
Independence	10 %
Special status	6 %
Sovereignty-association	2 %
No answer	5 %

As things stand today, 10 percent of the people in the rest of Canada would prefer that Quebec became an independent country. Support for this idea varies by region. It is highest in the Atlantic provinces (16 percent) and in the West (12 percent). In Ontario, 7 percent of the population would prefer to see

Quebec leave the federation. Assuming that about 75 percent of Canada's population is of voting age, this translates into an imposing base on which to build the Divestiture movement.

Region	Voting-Age Population	For Independence %	For Independence No. of Voters
Atlantic Provinces	1,811,000	16	290,000
Ontario	8,444,000	7	591,000
West	6,682,000	12	802,000

Total number of *Canadians* of voting age whose
preferred option for Quebec is independence   1,683,000

This is a much bigger base than the one Marcel Chaput started with in 1960.

There is additional good news for supporters of Divestiture in the Environics survey. Only 8 percent of Canadians outside Quebec are in favour of giving that province a preferred position within our constitutional structures, be it special status or sovereignty-association. Almost four of every five *Canadians* think that Quebec should accept its present status within Canada. Four out of five francophone Quebecers will never accept this.

In general, the current supporters of Quebec's independence in the rest of Canada are slightly younger, poorer, and less well educated than the population in general. It is tempting to assume that their reasons are based on a belief that they would be better off economically if Quebec were no longer around. They probably think that Quebec is taking more from the federation than it is contributing. This is true, but it's not the basis for our project and it will be important to make this clear from the beginning. Building up resentment against Quebec is the easy way – it's also the wrong way.

The critics of Divestiture will have two main objections. First, they will argue that we are being unfair and mean-spirited toward the francophone community, perhaps even bigoted. They will also suggest that the separation process will prove to be very costly for *Canada* as well as for Quebec. On the first issue we can be unequivocal. It is our present policies, and certainly the accommodations which would be necessary to satisfy Quebec, that are unfair to every other ethnic and cultural group in the country. It's not bigoted to insist that no ethnic community is entitled to special status in this country.

On the issue of costs, there is no way to calculate the price that is being paid for the current political uncertainty and there's no way to know exactly how much it will cost to end it. But recent studies are starting to show how the process can be successfully managed. And, as pointed out earlier, there are reasons to believe that *Canada* would be more prosperous after Divestiture. But at heart the issue is not about money. It's about a political fault line that runs straight through the civil association which must be understood and accepted by *Canadians* if their country is to be true to all its citizens – and to itself.

It's perhaps time to resurrect a book published twenty years ago, before Quebec's first referendum, by Jane Jacobs, titled *The Question of Separatism: Quebec and the Struggle over Sovereignty.*[2] Ms. Jacobs is not a political scientist, but her clarity of mind and her generosity have never been questioned. She argues against special status for Quebec within Canada: "It is easy to understand why even federalists in Quebec believe their province must possess these disproportionate powers – relative to the other provinces – but the fact remains that they would be disproportionate and that they would affect many matters of vital interest to Canadians outside Quebec."[3] Thus she argues for Quebec independence and a subsequent relationship which would "keep only the connections Quebec and the

rest of Canada would need to trade with each other and coop-
erate on projects of mutual interest."[4] Using the example of
Norway's secession from Sweden in 1905, Jacobs goes on to
suggest ways in which Quebec might be separated from the rest
of Canada. The book is devoid of any trace of bitterness toward
Quebec. It does not count the economic costs and benefits. Ms.
Jacobs simply argues, as we do, that the two political visions are
incompatible.

The first objective of the Divestiture movement will be simply
to make the idea respectable, to have it seen as one reasonable
and realistic alternative to be added to the others which are currently being considered. Once this has been accomplished, new
converts to the cause of Divestiture will be won with every
victory of a separatist government or a Bloc Québécois member
of Parliament, every effort by Quebec's Liberal Party to obtain
special status, every diplomatic squabble between Quebec and
Ottawa, every attack on the federal government by either
Quebec party, and every concession by Ottawa to the nationalist
movement. *Canadians* will no longer be faced with the frustra-
tion of waiting to find out what Quebecers are going to do, and
then reacting. They will have their own option and they will feel
better for having it.

At some point the idea will be picked up by Canada's political parties. It could begin in a provincial legislature. In Ottawa,
the Bloc Québécois might be expected to endorse Divestiture.
However, the federal Liberals, the only other party with a
Quebec power base, will oppose the project from beginning to
end, for two very good reasons. First, the Quebecers in this
party are committed to Quebec within Canada. With few exceptions they like the country the way it is, they believe the system
has been fair to Quebec, and their support for special status is
mainly tactical. They are among the 30 percent of Quebec francophones who feel a real attachment to their country. Secondly,

on a more practical level, they have the most to lose. At the time of writing, 26 of their 156 seats in the House of Commons are from Quebec constituencies.

Divestiture must find its initial roots in one of the three opposition parties – Reform, NDP, or Conservative – and the key to success lies in the province of Ontario. This is where the movement must begin. The Liberals are overwhelmingly powerful in Ontario. So the three opposition parties, with significant existing support for Divestiture within their own ranks in the West and the Maritimes, would have nothing to lose by experimenting with the idea in Canada's largest province. It can be presented as a pragmatic solution to Canada's National Unity crisis, one which will bring finality to the debate. It is not obvious that such an appeal would fall on deaf ears.

The experience of the separatist movement reminds us that this will not be a one-way street. Until it happens, Divestiture is something you can be in favour of on Monday and opposed to a week later. For instance, if a Quebec government were to sign the Canadian Constitution as it is, and welcome anglophones as full partners in their province, there would be no more need for the movement. But until that day it will be a permanent, respectable option for *Canadians*. It proposes a positive vision of the country which permits us to plan our future without agonizing over our many failings in the eyes of Quebec nationalists, or waiting to see what the next Quebec election will bring.

To those who believe that Quebec nationalism is disappearing, we will ask "How long are you prepared to wait?" Those who say the unity debate is good for us will be shown that they are being exploited. Those who think we should learn to live with the problem will be shown that it's too costly. The fatalists will be shown that they can, at last, take charge of their own political future.

The separatist experience in Quebec suggests that progress on the Divestiture idea may be slow. But there is another, more promising precedent: Czechoslovakia. In June 1990, support in Czech lands for the separation of Slovakia stood at 6 percent. By July 1992 it had risen to 16 percent. In September of that year it rose to 46 percent. Slovakia became independent on January 1, 1993.[5]

18

How Can Quebec Be Removed from the Federation?

It would be helpful to the process if Quebecers would agree to leave Canada quickly and quietly, but this cannot be guaranteed in advance. There are many precedents for secession in the literature of political science, but very few for Divestiture. Malaysia effectively divested itself of Singapore in 1965 and the underlying cause was ethnic conflict. The Czech-Slovak split in 1993 also had some of the characteristics of a Divestiture. Robert Young describes the two experiences in his book. These examples, like that of Norway, are suggestive, but none of them can serve as a manual for our project.

There is one example of Divestiture closer to home. The British, along with the other colonial powers, disentangled themselves from a number of costly dependencies after the Second World War, and one of these adventures directly affected Canada. Newfoundland became our tenth province in 1949 and the process was started by the unwillingness of the British to continue transfer payments to that Dominion. Raymond Blake in his book *Canadians at Last*[1] puts it this way: "The British government sought even the smallest signal that Canada was interested in Newfoundland. . . . As London turned its attention to post-war reconstruction, Newfoundland threatened to become a financial liability, especially after the Commission of Government presented a ten-year reconstruction plan in September 1944, estimated to cost the British $100 million. Britain could scarcely keep itself solvent; it could not afford scarce dollars to rehabilitate Newfoundland. The best solution would be union between Canada and Newfoundland."[2]

A referendum was arranged and Canada's Prime Minister Mackenzie King said (in a statement which sounds a bit like a Supreme Court ruling fifty years later) that Newfoundland would be accepted in Canada "should they make their decision clear and beyond all possibility of misunderstanding."[3] He settled for 52.34 percent.

For those with vivid imaginations, Britain's Divestiture of Newfoundland suggests the possibility that another country might be willing to take Quebec off our hands. France is the obvious prospect. For one thing, Paris, as a national capital, would be much better equipped than Ottawa to ensure a permanent respect for the French language and culture. However, it is unlikely that Quebecers could be persuaded to go along with such a project, even at the level of 52.34 percent, and it's even more unlikely that Washington would permit the creation of a *département* of the French Republic on its border. To achieve Divestiture it will be necessary for Quebec, like Singapore, Slovakia, and Norway, to become an independent country.

So once *Canadians* have decided that they want Quebec out of the federation it will be preferable to convince that province to leave. In fact the two processes will probably take place simultaneously. The very existence of a serious Divestiture movement in the rest of Canada could stimulate Quebecers to rethink their position. It could even create a change in public opinion, although it's not clear what this would be. Some observers have suggested that it will encourage separatism because it will be seen as an insult to the dignity of the Quebec people – "They are telling us we're not wanted, let's get out of here." Others think that there will be an opposite reaction, similar to the second thoughts which often arise when an unfaithful spouse is told to get out of the house. In this scenario, Quebec federalists would argue that they have been misunderstood.

In either event, a vigorous independence movement already exists in Quebec and we can assume from the public-opinion polls that about 30 percent of its population might approve the Divestiture project as presented, one which offers free trade but no political ties with Canada. The challenge is to find the other 25 percent. They must come from two groups among the ranks of francophone nationalists: first, the supporters of sovereignty-association who tend to vote "Yes" to the complicated questions that are concocted for Quebec referendums; and second, the ardent supporters of special status in all its variations, who tend to vote "No." With only 20 percent of Quebec's population willing to accept the constitutional status quo one might assume that acceptance of the Divestiture project would be easily obtained. However, it's not that simple. The 20 percent in question includes some very important people.

The first thing to do is make it crystal clear that, if Quebec is to remain in the federation, it must, once and for all, forget the dreams it may have of obtaining any kind of special status. The *Canadian* people don't want it. The latest figures indicate that 92 percent of them are opposed. It is time for our leaders to stop misleading Quebecers with foolish and meaningless declarations on the subject. Constitutionally speaking, if Quebec is to remain in Canada, its status will remain the same as Nova Scotia's.

This declaration, when fully understood and accepted in Quebec, should stimulate the Divestiture movement. It will incite some prominent nationalist intellectuals to announce that they have been converted to the cause of independence. Claude Castonguay and Claude Ryan can be counted on to write extended articles in the daily newspapers giving solid reasons for their change of heart. Other federalist nationalists will follow them. Unfortunately, they will not win everyone to their cause. For most of Quebec's francophone elite there is nothing to be gained by the loss of the "status" which is most precious to them – the "status quo." However, for less privileged voters, the end of a dream that was fashioned for them after the Laurendeau-Dunton report[4] in 1965 should bring a considerable number around to the cause of independence.

On the other hand, if Quebec goes along with our Divestiture project it has to be made clear that the new nation must forget about any possibility of political association with *Canada*. It appears that about 40 percent of the "Yes" vote in the 1995 referendum was made up Quebecers for whom separation was only acceptable if accompanied by such an association. Faced with the clear loss of this option, the separatist leaders will have to argue that it is not really necessary after all. The federal government, for the first time, will not contradict them. In fact, if *Canadians* are committed to Divestiture, their government might be expected to seek ways to reinforce the separatist position. This will produce some additional support, impossible to quantify, for unconditional secession.

Will the gains from those who must abandon any hope of special status make up for the loss of those who fear sovereignty without association? It's too close to call at this time, but for once the *Canadian* federalists and the Quebec separatists will have the same objective and can convey messages which do not conflict.

A widely supported Divestiture project will necessitate a major policy revision by both of Quebec's political parties. The Parti Québécois will have to concoct an independence proposal without a hyphen, one which acknowledges that the idea of a concurrent political association with Canada is dead. Their inventiveness in these matters should not be underestimated.

Things will be more difficult for the Quebec Liberal Party. They will be faced with a clear statement by the rest of Canada: no special status – ever. This will leave the Liberals with three choices. They could accept *Canada*'s clarification of its position and attempt to convince Quebec voters that Canada, with its present Constitution, is a good arrangement. If they were successful there might be no further need for Divestiture. Or the Liberals might become a second separatist party. This would go a long way to making Divestiture acceptable in Quebec. Or they could continue to seek special status while maintaining a policy of systematic obstruction of every federal initiative, and of every effort at constitutional reform. Over time, this would probably strengthen the Divestiture movement in the rest of Canada. It's also possible that the Quebec Liberal Party could break up over this issue.

In any event, a successful and coherent Divestiture movement is going to give Quebecers and their political leaders a lot to think about.

If Divestiture came to be supported by a majority of *Canadians*, and Quebecers did not want to leave, could they be obliged to do so? Perhaps. In 1998 the Supreme Court looked into the opposite possibility, the right of Quebec to secede against the wishes of *Canadians*, and seemed to go along with the idea. Starting from a declaration that "the Constitution is not a straitjacket," the ruling (paraphrased) reads as follows: "The continued existence and operation of the Canadian constitutional order could not be indifferent to a clear expression of a clear majority of *Canadians* that they no longer *wished* Quebec to remain in Canada. *Quebec* would have no basis to deny the right of the *governments of the rest of Canada* to pursue *Divestiture,* should a clear majority of the people of *the rest of Canada* choose that goal, so long as in doing so, *Canadians respect* the rights of others."[5]

If Quebecers are close to agreeing with the Divestiture project, but still hesitating, there remains the possibility of a buyout. Readers will recall that Quebec receives about $3 billion per year in services that *Canadians* are paying for. As a last resort, and a final incentive, it might be worthwhile to consider a one-time payment equal, say, to three times Quebec's annual deficit with the federal government. This would help Quebec, the smaller country, to cover some of the initial costs of its new status, and it would be relatively inexpensive for *Canada* in the long run, particularly in light of the future that awaits us once we are freed from the yoke of ethnic nationalism.

A Matter of the Heart

I'd like to take a final look at where this journey has brought us.

Respect for diversity has been imposed on *Canada* as a defining feature of our political structures for two reasons. The first is our size. The country is a ribbon of people, a "Chile laid on its side," stretching through six time zones and every kind of topography imaginable. *Canada* has been made even more diverse by the origins and cultures of the people who have settled here, and continue to do so – our fellow citizens. We, or our ancestors, left other countries where we were victims, to varying degrees, of prejudice and privilege, whether ethnic, linguistic, or religious. Sometimes these prejudices took the form of physical oppression. More often they expressed themselves as constraints imposed by the political and social order in these countries. We decided to leave all this for a New World, and have become *Canadians*.

The only kind of political regime that is workable and acceptable for *Canada* in such a situation is one which recognizes this diversity by being blind to it. Rights and responsibilities are attached to you and me as individuals. From that base we are free to propose common values and group ourselves into differing communities of our own choosing – and to abandon them – as we wish. The essential counterpart to this right is that it must be accorded to all on an equal basis. And so it is – with one exception. We have, somewhat reluctantly, agreed to make a special pact, whose details are still being worked out, with the native people. Everyone else, no matter what kind of community they wish to attach themselves to, must be treated equally. Religious groups, language groups, minorities of various persuasions, it doesn't matter, all are free to pursue their own agendas because the state "has no purpose of its own to defend against such community purposes." And none of these groups has the right to a privileged position within our Constitution.

These principles are identified with the name by which most *Canadians* understand them – fairness. They are the basis of a "civil association" and it's the only political association that can withstand the pressures and the ideologies of all the interest groups in this country. It is my belief that it's the only kind of system which is worth putting to the test of time.

Quebecers, francophone Quebecers, have never accepted this system. They believe that, as a linguistic and ethnic community, they have a right to a constitutionally based privileged position within the country. They see themselves as a different kind of "native people." They have created their own reservation where political life is based on a different concept of justice. And they also believe that their representation in the power structures of our whole country must be not just as one of ten provinces – or one of five voters – but, often, as one of two nations.

To a remarkable extent they have succeeded in this endeavour. Instinctively, francophone federalists and separatists have fashioned a "one-two" punch, which has staggered the rest of the country and keeps it reeling. First the separatists threaten secession, then the federalist elite exploits this possibility to force more concessions from *Canada* while appealing for generosity of spirit and reminding us of the obligation to redeem historical injustices. There is also an implied promise that someday this will all come to an end. But I believe it won't, because it's a system that works to perfection, for Quebec's francophone elite at least. It's their ultimate non-tariff barrier.

The rest of Canada should not put up with this any longer. It is being mugged, of course, but that's not the main reason to call a halt. What's going on is wrong in principle. *Canadian* academics and journalists are working overtime to find ways to make us feel guilty about our unwillingness to satisfy Quebec's aspirations when there is absolutely no practical or moral reason to do so. The Two Nations theory was always a doubtful hypothesis. The composition of our country now makes it both inapplicable and irrelevant.

Unless *Canada* takes action on this issue, it will never be resolved. And by doing something about it, *Canadians* provide themselves with a very important psychological bonus. They take their future into their own hands. They put an end to years of waiting to find out what Quebec's next demand will be and then living through a gut-wrenching debate over whether it can and should be satisfied. With Divestiture *Canadians* at last can say "Here's what we want; you reply."

The creation of a strongly supported Divestiture movement does not ensure that Quebec will agree to leave the federation. But the idea already has the support of at least a third of its population. This is a promising base to build on. And if both sides want Divestiture there is evidence, and there are some precedents, to indicate that it might be accomplished quickly and inexpensively.

This is a summary of the arguments in the book. And I think I have defended the logic of it all. But for a long time after I had these beliefs organized in my head they still didn't leave me satisfied. The heart kept getting in the way.

My thoughts kept going back to a warm and sunny October afternoon in 1997, after a football game at Bishop's University in Lennoxville, Quebec, where I spent my college years. We had beaten McGill, there were many friends in the stands, the leaves were brilliant in red and yellow, and the air was just at the point where you're not even aware that there is a temperature.

Walking back to the car with my dear friend Tony Abbott we got to talking about Quebec politics and the possibility of separation and how, if it came to pass, an afternoon like this one would be impossible. We couldn't find a way to put it in words but we both felt we'd be losing something important. A lot of Canadians, in Quebec and elsewhere, feel the same way. Even if you explain, and they finally accept in their heads, that separation or Divestiture does not mean the break-up of the country, there remains something, intangible, but more than a dream, a feeling of family perhaps, which seems to be violated.

Later that evening, driving back to Montreal, I tried to figure out what my heart was trying to tell me. What would be different if Quebec were not a part of Canada? The weather and the colours of the leaves would not change. Bishop's would still be there and Tony and I would still be free to visit the place as often as we liked. McGill could always be counted on to provide an endless supply of losing football teams. Bishop's University would have to change, to adapt to its new situation, but it has made many other changes successfully over its 150 years.

Yes, many of the English people who were there that afternoon would leave Quebec, but Divestiture would just accelerate a process that was occurring inexorably in any event. There would still be enough of us around to fill the stands for the rest of our lives and I think it could be argued that nothing vital to the daily life of an English Quebecer would necessarily change just because the province became a country.

This is even more likely to be true in the rest of Canada. Most *Canadians* know about Quebec only from what they have learned in the news media or in conversation with their friends, or as tourists. It's not a personal issue.

But still, in English Quebec and the rest of the country there's a positive feeling about keeping the country together, which must be addressed by anyone who is proposing something as radical as Divestiture. There's a strong mythology here that underpins our instinctive reaction to such a proposal, regardless of its merits.

In a recent book, *Reflections of a Siamese Twin*, John Ralston Saul takes another stab at defining the *Canadian* identity in terms of its memories.[1] Early in the book Saul speaks of the importance of myth – "a marriage of the past and the present" – in all our lives. And he goes on to talk about change – "Those who successfully embrace change do so from the solid base of what they are. Reality and a healthy mythology are the key to change."[2] In his book he identifies quite a few of the myths that, he feels, have formed, or deformed, us.

I understand that some people will reject the idea of Divestiture for logical reasons, because they see another reality. They think that the constitutional crisis is about to end, or that it's good for us. But for the rest of the country, for those who think that Divestiture makes some kind of sense, it will be necessary find a "healthy mythology" to replace the current myths that colour our relations with the place called "Quebec."

I have found one that works for me. It takes me back to Europe where, a century ago, my ancestors made an even more profound break with the myths of their collective past and got in a boat bound for the New World. A new myth had captured them, the myth of a land of opportunity. And – here's the point – immigration to *Canada* based on this ideal continues unabated up to the present day. I believe that the people who come here are special, different from their brothers, sisters, and cousins who preferred to remain at home. I'm talking both about those who arrived in the eighteenth century and those who got here last week. I believe these people understand that they are cutting their ties with a homeland, with a familiar culture which was finding its expression in the state where they lived, to seek opportunity – equal opportunity. I think they deserve to find it here.

If they come to Quebec they find themselves in New France, a European-style nation-state, alive and well in the New World. But if they come to *Canada*, they have arrived in "America," and I'm not talking about the United States. It's the vision, the mythology, of immigrants that has defined that word, America. I think it's time for us to reclaim it for *Canadians*, too, as "the solid base of what we are." It belongs to us as much as it does to our southern neighbours and we have hesitated to apply it to ourselves for far too long. I think that the ideas that will flow from the idea of a distinct *Canada*, in America, can be the base for a very "healthy mythology." We can see it stirring already in the first, tentative, suggestions that it might be time to bring home our head of state.

So I'd like to put the question clearly. In your heart do you believe that the Constitution and the laws of your country should give special recognition to a single linguistic, cultural, and ethnic group, the French, now and forever? The laws of Quebec do this today, and francophone Quebecers will never accept the *Canadian* Constitution as legitimate until it, also, includes that recognition. I don't agree with them. This is a matter of principle. We're all immigrants here. I'll settle for the idea of "fairness" as a base on which to construct my advocacy of Divestiture. And as for myth, I'll take "America" – a vision of people from every part of the world, joined in a political association that transcends nationality, here in *Canada*. You can build on that.

Notes

CHAPTER 2

1. Reed Scowen, "Reflections on the Future of the English Language in Quebec," June, 1979.

CHAPTER 4

1. Government of Quebec, *Charter of the French Language* (Quebec: Publications du Québec), chapter C-11.
2. The Quiet Revolution is the name given to the secularization and modernization of Quebec's social, economic, and political life, which is generally considered to have begun with the election of the Liberal government of Jean Lesage in 1960.
3. Reed Scowen, *A Different Vision: The English in Quebec in the 1990s* (Toronto: Maxwell Macmillan Canada, 1991).
4. Assemblée Nationale du Québec, *Journal des débats*, December 20, 1988, p. 4452.
5. *Charter of the French Language*, preamble.

6. Claude Ryan, "Déclaration de Claude Ryan sur la politique lin-
   guistique," April 1978.
7. Claude Ryan, "Letter to My Fellow Citizens of Notre-Dame-de-
   Grâce," June 27, 1978. Essentially the same letter was written to
   voters in the riding of Argenteuil on April 16, 1978, during the by-
   election in which Ryan was a candidate.
8. See Resolution no. 5 adopted by the general council of the Quebec
   Liberal Party in June 1985.

CHAPTER 5

1. Statistics Canada, "1996 Census Nation Tables."
2. 1976 figures are from Statistics Canada, Language Unit, Housing,
   Family and Social Statistics Division, June 5, 1990.
3. This is my estimate. The 1996 census reveals that 664,500
   Quebecers were born outside Canada, including 27,130 born in the
   U.S.A., 20,910 in the United Kingdom, 67,370 in the Caribbean and
   Bermuda, and 62,510 in Africa. There appear to be no figures available on the birthplaces of interprovincial migrants living in
   Quebec. On July 1, 1995, there were 50,348 non-permanent residents in Quebec.
4. See note 6, chapter 4.
5. Alliance Quebec, "Brief Presented to the Special Joint Committee
   to Amend Section 93 of the Constitution Act, 1867 Concerning the
   Quebec School System," October 20, 1997.
6. In 1991 there were 402 French schools in Ontario and 353 English
   schools in Quebec. (Canada, Office of the Commissioner of
   Official Languages *Annual Report*, 1991.)
7. Government of Quebec, Ministère des Relations avec les Citoyens
   et de l'Immigration, "Guide des procédures de sélection." Regu-
   lation in effect September 15, 1993.
8. According to Statistics Canada, for the twelve months' period
   from July 1994 to June 1995, Quebec's share of Canadian immigration was 26,943 out of 215,652, or 12.4 percent.
9. See note 8, chapter 4.

10. Donald Macpherson, "A Chance to Hire Anglos," Montreal *Gazette*, August 20, 1997.

11. Government of Quebec, Ministère du Conseil Exécutif, "Liste integrée des sous-ministres, sous-ministres associés, secrétaires adjoints, sous-ministres adjoints ou assimilés," July 9, 1997.

12. See note 8, chapter 4.

13. Michael Hamelin et al., "Bad Medicine," Montreal *Gazette*, August 16, 1997.

14. Reed Scowen, *A Different Vision: The English in Quebec in the 1990s* (Maxwell Macmillan Canada 1991).

15. Donald Macpherson, "Good News for French," Montreal *Gazette*, December 13, 1997.

16. Comité sur l'évolution du federalisme Canadien, "Recognition and Interdependence" (Quebec Liberal Party, December 1996), proposal 56.

17. I recently received a call from my sister who lives in a farmhouse in Reedville in the Eastern Townships, a home built by our grandfather almost one hundred years ago. She was about to paint the barn behind the house and wanted to know if it would be legal for her to decorate the side of the building with the words "Reedville Farm." I called the local representative of Quebec's National Assembly, who called the Office of the French Language, who said it would be illegal to do that unless the words "Ferme Reedville" also appeared, in letters twice as large as the English version.

18. *Charter of the French Language*, preamble.

19. Ibid., article 4.

20. Jonathan Gatehouse, "OLF Petty, Excessive: Grey," Montreal *Gazette*, April 16, 1998.

21. Brief of the Conseil du Patronat to the Commission Parlementaire on Bill 1, Assemblée Nationale du Québec, June 1977. My translation.

CHAPTER 6

1. Canada, Task Force on Canadian Unity, *A Future Together* (Ottawa: The Queen's Printer, 1979).

2. Christopher Moore, *1867: How the Fathers Made a Deal* (Toronto: McClelland & Stewart, 1997), p. 159.

3. A recent and interesting account of the process is to be found in Moore's book (see note 2 above).

4. Quoted in Samuel V. LaSelva, *The Moral Foundations of Canadian Federalism* (Montreal: McGill-Queen's Press, 1996), p. 25.

5. Canada, Task Force on Canadian Unity, *A Future Together* (Ottawa: The Queen's Printer, 1979), Recommendation 28ii.

6. Ibid., Recommendation 33.

7. Ibid., Recommendation 34.

8. The Constitutional Committee of the Quebec Liberal Party, "A New Canadian Federation" (Quebec Liberal Party, January 9, 1980), p. 22.

9. Ibid.

10. Comité sur l'évolution du federalisme Canadien, "Recognition and Interdependence," chapter 4.

CHAPTER 7

1. Comité sur l'évolution du federalisme Canadien, "Recognition and Interdependence."

2. Ibid., chapter 1, p. 10.

3. Ibid., chapter 5, p. 56.

4. Ibid., chapter 4, p. 53.

5. Côté, Marcel, *Le Rêve de la terre promise* (Montreal: Les Éditions Stanké, 1995) p.219. My translation.

6. Lysiane Gagnon, "Two Arguments a Federalist Must Never Make," *Globe and Mail*, August 23, 1997.

7. Maurice Pinard, Robert Bernier, Vincent Lemieux, *Un Combat inachevé* (Sainte-Foy: Presses de l'Université du Québec, 1997).

8. Poll conducted by Environics and CROP. Details published in the newsletter of the Council for Canadian Unity, *Opinion Canada*, vol. 6, no. 3, June, 1998.

9. Poll conducted for *Le Devoir* by Sondagem between May 29 and June 2, 1998, and reported in the issue of June 23, 1998.

10. Maurice Pinard, "The Political Universe of Ambivalent Franco-phone Voters," *Opinion Canada*, vol. 6, no. 4, September 1998.
11. Pinard, Bernier, Lemieux, *Un Combat inachevé*, p.90.
12. Ibid., p. 342.

CHAPTER 8

1. Philip Resnick, *Thinking English Canada* (Toronto: Stoddart, 1994).
2. *World Development Report 1998–99* (Washington: The World Bank), table 1, p. 190.
3. Michael J. Sandel, *Democracy's Discontent* (Cambridge, Mass.: Harvard University Press, 1996).
4. Michael J. Sandel, "America's Search for a New Public Philosophy," *Atlantic Monthly*, March 1996. All quotes attributed to Sandel are from this article.
5. Michael Ignatieff, *Blood and Belonging* (Toronto: Penguin Books, 1994).
6. Elie Kedourie, *Nationalism* (London: Century Hutchison Ltd., 1986), p. 9.
7. Daniel Patrick Moynihan, *Pandaemonium: Ethnicity in International Politics* (New York: Oxford University Press, 1993). See in particular chapter 2 – "On the Self-Determination of Peoples."
8. Kedourie, *Nationalism*, p. 138.
9. Michael Oakeshott, *On Human Conduct* (Oxford: Oxford University Press, 1975), pp. 275–6 and 308.
10. Charles Taylor, *Multiculturalism and the Politics of Recognition* (Princeton: Princeton University Press, 1992), p. 58–61.
11. Charles Taylor, *Recognizing the Solitudes: Essays on Canadian Federalism and Nationalism* (Montreal: McGill-Queen's University Press, 1993), p. 181ff.
12. Ibid., p. 59.

CHAPTER 9

1. Bruce Hutchison, *The Unknown Country* (Toronto: Longmans, Green & Company, 1942).

2. Ibid., p. 4.

3. George Grant, *Lament for a Nation: The Defeat of Canadian Nationalism* (Toronto: McClelland & Stewart, 1965).

4. Richard Gwyn, *Nationalism Without Walls* (Toronto: McClelland & Stewart, 1996).

5. Seymour Martin Lipset, *Continental Divide: The Values and Institutions of the United States and Canada* (New York: Routledge, Chapman & Hall, 1990).

6. Ibid., p. 8.

7. In 1995, Canada spent $2,049 U.S. per person on health care. The U.S. spent $3,701. The private sector shares were Canada 28.2 percent, U.S.A. 53.5 percent. OECD figures from an article by Claude Picher, "Les Dépenses de santé," *La Presse* (Montreal), August 26, 1997.

8. J. L. Granatstein, *Yankee Go Home: Canadians and Anti-Americanism* (Toronto: HarperCollins, 1996).

CHAPTER 10

1. Statistics Canada, "1996 Census Nation Tables: Single and Multiple Ethnic Origin Responses." Without Quebec, Canada has a population of 21,483,000. Of this number, 621,000 say they are of French origin. From the British Isles, there are 3,099,000 people with a single origin (e.g. Welsh) and 1,561,000 people with multiple British Isles origins (e.g. English and Scottish). There is also a significant number of Canadians who claim multiple origins that include French or British Isles. They have not been included in my figures.

2. Geoffrey Nunberg, "Lingo Jingo: English Only and the New Nativism," *The American Prospect*, no.33, July-August 1997. Nunberg states that in the U.S.A. "the actual Census figure for residents over five who speak no English is only 1.9 million." According to the 1996 Canadian census figures there are 4,110,000 Quebecers and 526,000 Canadians in other provinces who speak no English.

3. Camille Laurin, "Quebec's Policy on the French Language" (Quebec: Ministère de la Culture et des Communications, 1977).

4. Statistics Canada, "1996 Census Nation Tables: Population by Knowledge of Official Language." 69.3 percent of Quebec's mother-tongue francophones – 3,951,710 out of a total of 5,700,150 – speak no English.

5. Statistics Canada, "1996 Census Nation Tables: Population by Home Language." 18,320,000 of the 21,483,000 residents of Canada outside Quebec have English as the "language spoken most often at home."

6. Ibid.

7. *Oxford English Dictionary*, 1971 edition, s.v. "culture."

8. Camille Laurin, "Quebec's Policy on the French Language."

9. The celebration of Quebec's National Day, June 24, is highlighted by a parade in Montreal, organized, with the approval of the Quebec government, by the Société St-Jean-Baptiste. This organization has its roots in the Roman Catholic Church and has become one of the most vocal proponents of Quebec's independence. Because many Quebecers are neither Catholics nor separatists, the preparations for the parade are preceded each year by a hilarious debate over the number of floats that will carry religious symbols, nationalist symbols, or Trinidadian steel bands. In 1998, the president of Alliance Quebec, the English-language rights group, was removed from the parade by police, "for his own safety."

10. Government of Quebec, "Rapport du comité interministériel sur la situation de la langue française," 1996, p. 239.

11. Ray Conlogue, *Impossible Nation: The Longing for Homeland in Canada and Quebec* (Stratford, Ont.: The Mercury Press, 1996).

CHAPTER 11

1. Supreme Court of Canada, "Reference re: Secession of Quebec," file no. 25506, para. 32, August 20, 1998.

2. Canada, Department of Justice, "The Constitution Acts 1867 to 1982." (Ottawa: The Queen's Printer, 1996).

3. Jeffrey Simpson, "The Rest of Canada Ponders Quebec," Occasional Paper no. 17. The Center for the Study of Canada, SUNY Plattsburgh, July 1998, p. 5.
4. Oakeshott, *On Human Conduct*, p. 201.
5. Aleksander Solzhenitsyn. Quoted in Moynihan (see note 7, chapter 8), p. 134.

CHAPTER 12

1. Comité sur l'évolution du federalisme Canadien, "Recognition and Interdependence," chapter 3, pp. 40–41.
2. See articles 41 and 42 of the Constitution Act.

CHAPTER 13

1. These statistics are taken from Robert A. Young, *The Secession of Quebec and the Future of Canada*, (Montreal: McGill-Queen's University Press, 1998), p. 10.
2. Côté, *Le Rêve de la terre promise.*
3. Ibid., p. 100.
4. A recent article by the economist Georges Mathews puts the figure at $4.6 billion for 1997–98. "Le régime de péréquation continue de favoriser largement le Québec," *La Presse* (Montreal), September 24, 1998.
5. Côté, *La Rêve de la terre promise*, p. 67.
6. Ibid., p. 61*ff.*
7. Ibid., p. 69*ff.*
8. Ibid., p. 72.

CHAPTER 14

1. See note 1, chapter 11.
2. Robert Young, *The Secession of Quebec and the Future of Canada* (Montreal: McGill-Queen's University Press, 1995), p. 313, note 1.
3. Ibid. These figures are taken from tables A1 and A2 of Young's book.

4. An extensive bibliography can be found on pages 343–367 of Young's book.
5. Young, p. 208*ff*.
6. Alan C. Cairns, "Looking into the Abyss: The Need for a Plan C," from *The Secession Papers* (Toronto: C. D. Howe Institute, September 1997), no. 96, p. 12.
7. Young, *The Secession of Quebec and the Future of Canada*, p. 13.

CHAPTER 15

1. Norman Webster, "Long Way to Go: Mean-Spirited Book Lacks a Vision of Canada," Montreal *Gazette*, August 17, 1991.
2. For additional information on the creation of Alliance Quebec and its activities, see my book *A Different Vision: The English in Quebec in the 1990s* (Toronto: Maxwell Macmillan Canada, 1991).
3. Statistics Canada, "1996 Census Nation Tables."
4. There are no statistics that neatly divide the anglophone community into the artificial categories which I have created for this analysis. The estimates for each category are mine, based on my knowledge of the community and the opinions of a number of informed observers who were consulted. For the purpose of these calculations I have used the census figures based on the language most frequently used in the home.

CHAPTER 16

1. See note 1, chapter 13.
2. Patrick J. Monahan and Michael J. Bryant, "Coming to Terms with Plan B." No. 83, June 1996.
   Alan C. Cairns, "Looking into the Abyss." No. 96, September 1997.
   Peter Russell and Bruce Ryder – "Ratifying a Postreferendum Agreement on Sovereignty." No. 97, October 1997.
   David Laidler and William B. P. Robson, "Walking the Tightrope." No. 102, March 1998.
   Richard Simeon, "Limits to Partnership." No. 104, March 1998.

3. Government of Quebec, Secrétariat à la Restructuration, *Sommaire des études sur la restructuration administrative* (Quebec: Publications du Québec, 1995).
4. See note 2, above: Simeon, "Limits to Partnership," p. 32.
5. The pages that follow summarize chapters 13 and 14 of Young's book.
6. Michel Demers and Marcel Côté, "Is UDI Feasible: The Economic Impact of a Conflict of Legitimacy," October 1997.

CHAPTER 17

1. "The Focus Canada Report," Environics Research Group, Toronto. Survey dates are June 20 – July 16, 1998.
2. Jane Jacobs, *The Question of Separatism: Quebec and the Struggle over Sovereignty* (New York: Random House, 1980).
3. Ibid., p. 81.
4. Ibid., p. 123.
5. Young, *The Secession of Quebec and the Future of Canada*, p. 148.

CHAPTER 18

1. Raymond R. Blake, *Canadians at Last: Canada Integrates Newfoundland as a Province* (Toronto: University of Toronto Press, 1994).
2. Ibid., p. 14.
3. Ibid., p. 12.
4. The Royal Commission on Bilingualism and Biculturalism, 1963–1971.
5. See chapter 11, note 1.

CHAPTER 19

1. John Ralston Saul, *Reflections of a Siamese Twin: Canada at the End of the Twentieth Century* (Toronto: Penguin Books, 1997).
2. Ibid., p. 10.

Selected Bibliography

The subjects of this book – Canadian identity, Quebec politics, nationalism, the civil association – have inspired an extensive body of work over many years. The short bibliography which follows is a list of the documents that I have found interesting, and often useful, in the preparation of *Time to Say Goodbye*. Many of the books I list here incorporate more complete bibliographies to which the student of these subjects can refer.

CANADA AND QUEBEC

Aquin, Hubert. *Writing Quebec: Selected Essays*. Edmonton: University of Alberta Press, 1988.

Bailey, A. G. *Culture and Nationality*. Toronto: McClelland & Stewart, 1972.

Bercuson, David J., and Barry Cooper. *Deconfederation: Canada Without Quebec*. Toronto: Key Porter Books, 1991.

Blake, Raymond B. *Canadians at Last: Canada Integrates Newfoundland as a New Province*. Toronto: University of Toronto Press, 1994.

Caldwell, Gary and Eric Waddell. *The English of Quebec*. Quebec City: ICRC, 1982.

Cameron, David. *Nationalism, Self-Determination and the Quebec Question*. Toronto: Macmillan of Canada, 1974.

Conlogue, Ray. *Impossible Nation*. Stratford, Ont.: The Mercury Press, 1996.

Cook, Ramsay. *The Maple Leaf Forever: Essays on Nationalism and Politics in Canada*. Toronto: Macmillan of Canada, 1971.

Cook, Ramsay, ed. *French Canadian Nationalism*. Toronto: Macmillan of Canada, 1971.

Côté, Marcel. *Le Rêve de la terre promise*. Montreal: Les Éditions Stanké, 1995.

Dion, Leon. *La Prochaine revolution*. Montreal: Leméac, 1973.

Dumont, Fernand. *The Vigil of Quebec*. Toronto: University of Toronto Press, 1971.

Ferguson, Will. *Why I Hate Canadians*. Vancouver: Douglas and McIntyre, 1997.

Francis, Daniel. *National Dreams: Myth, Memory, and Canadian History*. Vancouver: Arsenal Pulp Press, 1997.

Gibbens, Roger and Guy Laforest, ed. *Beyond the Impasse*. Montreal: IRPP, 1998.

Granatstein, J. L. *Yankee Go Home*. Toronto: HarperCollins, 1996.

Grant, George. *Lament for a Nation*. Toronto: McClelland & Stewart, 1970.

Gwyn, Richard. *Nationalism Without Walls*. Toronto: McClelland & Stewart, 1996.

Hutchison, Bruce. *The Unknown Country: Canada and Her People*. Toronto: Longmans, Green & Company, 1942

Jacobs, Jane. *The Question of Separatism: Quebec and the Struggle over Sovereignty*. Toronto: Random House, 1980.

Jedwab, Jack. *English in Montreal*. Montreal: Les Éditions Images, 1996.

Johnson, Daniel. *Egalité ou indépendence*. Montreal: Éditions Renaissance, 1965.

Johnson, William. *A Canadian Myth*. Montreal: Robert Davies, 1994.

Joy, Richard. *Languages in Conflict*. Published by the author, Ottawa 1967.

LaSelva, Samuel V. *The Moral Foundations of Canadian Federalism*. Montreal: McGill-Queen's University Press, 1996.

Laurendeau, André. *Witness for Quebec*. Toronto: Macmillan of Canada, 1973.

Lévesque, René. *Memoirs*. Montreal: Éditions Quebec/Amerique, 1986.

Lipset, Seymour Martin. *Continental Divide*. New York: Routledge, 1990.

Meekison, J. Peter. *Canadian Federalism, Myth or Reality*, third ed. Toronto: Methuen, 1977.

Moore, Christopher. *1867: How the Fathers Made a Deal*. Toronto: McClelland & Stewart, 1997.

Morchain, Janet Kerr and Mason Wade. *Search for a Nation: French-English Relations in Canada Since 1759*. Toronto: J. M. Dent & Sons, 1967.

Morton, Desmond. *A Short History of Canada*. Toronto: McClelland & Stewart, 1997.

Pinard, Maurice, Robert Bernier and Vincent Lemieux. *Un Combat inachevé*. Montreal: Presses de l'Université du Quebec, 1997.

Reid, Scott. *Lament for a Notion*. Vancouver: Arsenal Pulp Press, 1993.

Resnick, Philip. *Thinking English Canada*. Toronto: Stoddart, 1994.

Ryan, Claude. *Une Société stable*. Montreal: Éditions Heritage, 1978.

Saul, John Ralston. *Reflections of a Siamese Twin*. Toronto: Penguin Books, 1997.

Scowen, Reed. *A Different Vision: The English in Quebec in the 1990s*. Toronto: Maxwell Macmillan Canada, 1991.

Taylor, Charles. *Reconciling the Solitudes*. Montreal: McGill-Queen's Press, 1993.

Trudeau, Pierre Elliott. *Federalism and the French Canadians*. Toronto: Macmillan of Canada, 1968.

Underhill, Frank H. *The Image of Confederation*. CBC, Ottawa 1970.

Vallières, Pierre. *White Niggers of America*. Toronto: McClelland & Stewart, 1971.

Young, Robert A. *The Secession of Quebec and the Future of Canada.* Montreal: McGill-Queen's University Press, 1998.

NATIONALISM AND THE CIVIL ASSOCIATION

Anderson, Benedict. *Imagined Communities.* London: Verso Editions, 1983.

Barbalet, J. M. *Citizenship.* Milton Keynes, England: Open University Press, 1988.

Berlin, Isaiah. *The Sense of Reality: Studies in Ideas and Their History.* New York: Farrar, Strauss and Giroux, 1996.

Carr, E. H. *Nationalism and After.* London: Macmillan, 1968.

Courchene, Thomas J., ed. *The Nation State in a Global/Information Era: Policy Challenges.* Kingston, Ont.: Queen's University, 1997.

Dahrendorf, Ralf. *Reflections on the Revolution in Europe.* New York: Random House, 1990.

Dahrendorf, Ralf. *The Modern Social Conflict.* London: Weidenfield and Nicholson, 1988.

Deutsch, Karl W. *Nationalism and Social Communication.* Boston: M.I.T. Press, 1966.

Friedman, Thomas L. *From Beirut to Jerusalem.* New York: Doubleday, 1995.

Gellner, Ernest. *Nations and Nationalism.* Oxford: Basil Blackwell, 1990.

Heater, Derek. *Citizenship.* London: Longman, 1990.

Hinsley, F. H. *Sovereignty.* Cambridge: Cambridge University Press, 1989.

Hobsbawm, E. J. *Nations and Nationalism Since 1780.* Cambridge: Cambridge University Press, 1990.

Ignatieff, Michael. *Blood and Belonging.* Toronto: Penguin Books, 1993.

Isaacs, Harold R. *Idols of the Tribe.* New York: Harper & Row, 1975.

Kedourie, Elie. *Nationalism.* London: Century Hutchison, 1986.

Kohr, Leopold. *The Breakdown of Nations.* New York: E. P. Dutton, 1978.

Kristeva, Julia. *Nations Without Nationalism.* New York: Columbia University Press, 1993.

Minogue, K. R. *Nationalism*. London: Methuen and Co., 1969.

Moynihan, Daniel Patrick. *Pandaemonium: Ethnicity in International Politics*. New York: Oxford University Press, 1993.

Oakeshott, Michael. *On Human Conduct*. Oxford: Clarendon Press, 1975.

Oakeshott, Michael. *Rationalism in Politics and Other Essays*. London: Methuen and Co., 1974.

Olson, Mancur. *The Rise and Decline of Nations*. New Haven: Yale University Press, 1982.

Pfaff, William. *The Wrath of Nations*. New York: Simon and Schuster, 1993.

Rabushka, Alvin and Kenneth A. Shepsle. *Politics in Plural Societies*. Columbus, Ohio: Charles E. Merrill, 1972.

Rocker, Rudolph. *Nationalism and Culture*. Montreal: Black Rose Books, 1998.

Said, Edward W. *Culture and Imperialism*. New York: Vintage Books, 1994.

Sandel, Michael J. *Democracy's Discontent*. Cambridge, Mass.: Harvard University Press, 1996.

Schlesinger, Arthur M., Jr. *The Disuniting of America: Reflections on a Multicultural Society*. New York: W. W. Norton, 1992.

Smith, Anthony D. *Nationalism in the Twentieth Century*. Oxford: Martin Robertson, 1979.

Taylor, Charles. *Multiculturalism and the Politics of Recognition*. Princeton: Princeton University Press, 1992.

Acknowledgements

I have received invaluable advice from a number of people in the course of preparing the book. In recognizing them here I want to make it clear that no one has endorsed my proposition – no one has been asked to do so. But the book has been enriched by the suggestions of Tony Abbott, Richard Beach, Tom Birks, Anne Bohm, Shirley Braverman, David Cameron, Marcel Côté, Charles Doran, Martha and Peter Duffield, Jim Ferrabee, Gordon Gibson, Michael Goldbloom, Julius Grey, Tony Griffiths, John Hallward, Brian Levitt, Phil O'Brien, Donald Macdonald, Juta Reed, Cynthia Ryan, Peter Scowen, Charles Taylor, Gerald Tremblay, Norman Webster, and Robert Young. My sincere thanks to them.

I would also like to acknowledge the very special influence of Bill Letwin and the late Michael Oakeshott at the London School of Economics on the way I see the political landscape, and life itself. Their particular qualities of wisdom and friendship have touched me profoundly.

And thanks to Linda McKnight, Jonathan Webb, and Lisan Jutras, who helped me turn a text into a book.